MASTER YOUR CASH FLOW

Advance Praise for ***Master Your Cash Flow***

"This is a smart book for smart people! With a clever focus on tax strategies, this book is a great resource for anyone asking, 'Where did all my money go?' at the end of every month. Whether you're buried in student debt or just starting to build wealth, these strategies will help you keep more of what you earn."
—**Nicole Lapin**, *New York Times* bestselling author, founder of Money News Network, and host of the *Money Rehab* podcast

"What I appreciate most about this book is that it connects money to real life. It is not just about numbers. It is about freedom, peace of mind, and having a plan that supports the way you actually want to live. That makes it both practical and powerful."
—**David Bach**, 10x *New York Times* bestselling author, including #1 *New York Times* bestseller *The Automatic Millionaire* & *The Latte Factor*

"*Master Your Cash Flow* does what so many personal finance books fail to do: It connects financial decisions with how people actually live their lives. Most personal finance books targeted at millennials and younger readers fall into one of two camps: They either dilute key financial concepts but lack practical steps people can actually take, or they get too prescriptive and forget the human side of money. *Master Your Cash Flow* avoids both of these mistakes. Al and Amin offer a practical roadmap for understanding cash flow, making better financial decisions, and building wealth, while also addressing the psychological and emotional issues that impact how people think about money.

This book cuts through the complexity of ideas and encourages you to be more intentional, informed, and confident with your personal finances. It is a meaningful, actionable guide for anyone who wants more clarity,

less financial stress, and a smarter way to build wealth, and enjoy life in the present. If you're serious about taking control of your money and building wealth, this is the education you've been looking for."
—**Lou Tzamalas, CFP®, CPA, CAP®, EA, CFP®** Instructor & Subject Matter Expert, Boston University

"As a musician navigating multiple projects, irregular income, and the beautiful chaos of a creative career, I thought I had a working relationship with money. *Master Your Cash Flow* showed me I had something closer to an avoidance strategy. With warmth and zero condescension, Al and Amin replace financial anxiety with something far more useful: a clear, actionable framework for making better decisions without giving up the life you're actually living.

For artists, freelancers, and anyone whose income doesn't arrive in a neat, predictable envelope, this book is essential reading. Al and Amin have taught me that discipline and joy are not opposites. Turns out, that's exactly what this book is all about."
—**Kristhyan Benitez**, Concert Pianist, Steinway Artist, Latin Grammy Winner, Composer

"There is a moment early in *Master Your Cash Flow* that really stayed with me. It is quiet, honest, and very real, a moment where everything feels like it could fall apart. It captures a fear that many people carry but rarely say out loud. What follows is not just a story of recovery, but a practical path forward. Al and Amin take that vulnerability and turn it into something useful, showing how better financial decisions can rebuild not only wealth, but confidence and peace of mind. It is a powerful reminder that it is never too late to take control and change the direction of your financial life."
—**Hamid Mokhneche**, President, Film Production, Tyrus Pictures, LLC, Los Angeles, Miami, Paris

"Most personal finance books read like punishment: cut the latte, skip the dinner, defer the life. Al Zdenek and Amin Boroomand have written the opposite book—and it is the one most of us actually need. *Master Your Cash Flow* makes a quietly radical case: you do not need to be born wealthy to live wealthily. You need to make the right decisions, again and again, and let compounding do what it does. The book is the proof that the rest of us can achieve what we want financially but live the life we want along the way."

—**Eva Platini-Hernandez**, VP Business Development, WHP Global

"This book was a real eye-opener for me. I already had a basic strategy for putting any savings or extra cash to work after paying down debt. But what was missing, grossly missing, was a clear set of goalposts. We didn't have a real plan, and we didn't have the habit of making financial decisions based on long-term goals or our actual cash flow situation. The book exposed the gap between having good intentions and having an actual financial system in place. It gave us the insight we needed to truly understand what building wealth really means. Now, thanks to those lessons, we're on our way to building a financial future that supports the life we truly want to live."

—**Tamar Jean Baptiste-Lapoterie**, Finance Executive, Infrastructure, Fintech & Strategic Operations

"There is no shortage of financial advice out there, but much of it feels either overwhelming or difficult to apply in real life. What I found refreshing about this book is how clear and practical it is. The ideas are not just theoretical. They actually help you make better informed financial decisions day to day. Al and Amin bring a sense of clarity to something that often feels confusing, and with that clarity comes confidence. It goes beyond being a financial guide. It gives you a way to think about your money so you can take control of the life you want to live."

—**Richard Cancro**, Transforming Financial Experiences, CEO & Founder AdvisorEngine

"Everyone has a relationship to money, and perhaps you've just never been shown how to make the right financial decisions. Reading about how small financial decisions can have a ripple effect on your long-term wealth can fundamentally rewire your thinking and that is what makes *Master Your Cash Flow* so valuable. It breaks things down in a way that is easy to understand and actually usable. What stands out is how practical it is. It does not ask you to give up the things you enjoy, but instead, shows you how to make smarter choices with what you already have. Over time, this creates less stress, more clarity, and a real sense that financial freedom is something you can actually reach. This is a must read!"
—**Bari Zahn, Esq.**, Founder & Managing Partner,
Zahn Law Global, LLP

"Most personal finance books try to get you fired up. This one just shows you how money actually works. The spending plan reframe alone is worth the read. I've gone through this manuscript more times than I can count, and the thing that sticks with me is how practical it is. No hype, no guilt trips, just a clear process you can start using the same week you pick it up."
—**Jimi Gibson**, VP Brand Communications, Thrive Agency

"An incredibly honest and inspiring look at how financial struggles can be transformed into lasting success with the right guidance and mindset. The authors make complex financial concepts feel approachable, showing that anyone—regardless of background—can learn to master their cash flow and build a better future. I especially appreciated the emphasis on personal responsibility paired with practical, non-intimidating steps that reduce fear and overwhelm. The real-life stories add depth and relatability, proving that financial freedom is achievable, not just theoretical. Overall, this is a motivating and empowering start that gives readers both hope and a clear path forward."
—**Richard ("Rick") W. Weyers**, Vice President, Mercer Advisors, Inc.

"This is honestly one of the most engaging and refreshing books I've read on personal finance. Al and Amin have an incredible way of turning what is normally a stressful or intimidating subject into something genuinely enjoyable, motivating, and easy to connect with. The humor, storytelling, and honesty give the book real personality, while the ideas themselves are practical, clear, and surprisingly powerful. It never feels preachy or overly corporate—it feels human.

What resonated with me most was the idea that building a meaningful life and building financial security do not have to be in conflict with each other. For people who are driven by passion, creativity, and purpose in their work, that message is incredibly important. Al and Amin show that better financial decisions can actually create more freedom, confidence, and peace of mind, allowing people to focus more fully on the life and work they care about most. The whole book feels optimistic, empowering, and deeply relevant to the way many people want to live today."
—**Daniel Le**, Concert Pianist, Educator, Australia, SG and USA

I've spent my career building businesses where cash flow discipline is everything. Most individuals never get taught to think about money that way. This book closes that gap—it gives you a clear, practical way to understand where your money is going and how to make better decisions with it."
—**Zain Jaffer**, Founder of Vungle ($780M exit to Blackstone), CEO of Zain Ventures

"Al and Amin are wise beyond words. Their understanding of how to accumulate wealth is both illuminating and, surprisingly, comforting. That's because they have been real partners in unfolding the financial future I always desired but couldn't create on my own. I not only learned how to generate financial wealth, but also learned that "real wealth" meant having an abundance of all things I value: independence, love,

health, etc. If you are looking for the key to unlock a sense of financial freedom in your life, you will love this book."
—**David Zelman PhD**, Founder & CEO, Transitions Institute, Inc.

"Al and Amin don't just explain personal finance; they show you exactly how to take control of your cash flow, reduce the fear and anxiety behind financial decisions, and build a life you genuinely want to live. There are insights in this book that can truly change the trajectory of your life—and, more importantly, they are practical and immediately applicable. This book doesn't just change the way you think about money; it changes and expands the way you live."

"I love their brilliance in breaking complex ideas down into something simple and actionable. The reflective questions throughout the book create real awareness, and the way it's written makes it easy to understand while inspiring you to expand your vision for your life."
—**David Medina**, Executive Coach & Trusted Advisor, Partnering With Visionary Leaders On Their Journey To Excellence

"Over more than three decades building biotechnology and pharmaceutical companies, I have worked alongside some of the brightest scientists in the world, brilliant, hardworking people who bring extraordinary rigor to the most complex problems in human biology, yet who have rarely been offered that same rigor when it comes to their own finances. *Master Your Cash Flow* finally closes that gap. The rare pairing of Al Zdenek's four decades of financial wisdom with Amin Boroomand's analytical mind as a young PhD scientist produces a book that respects the reader's intelligence and translates wealth-building into something a scientist can actually use. I wish I could place this book into the hands of every young researcher I have ever mentored. They deserve financial freedom, and the world needs them to have it so they can stay focused on solving humanity's biggest problems."
—**Dr. Bijan Almassian**, President & CEO, Viridion Therapeutics

"Expert advice on finances is plentiful, and some of it is useful. Al and Amin are evangelists and bring something quite different with their in-depth expertise. The insights and methodologies they bring to helping their reader take control of their finances is a moving testament to their deep-seated commitment.

The methodologies they bring at times differ dramatically from standard advice focusing on maintaining an enjoyable and, in fact, joyful life while saving and investing. They tell rich and revealing stories of everyday people facing situations that most of us have experienced throughout our life. Yet they reframe the gym membership, the course, the flight to see family you love, all of it, as part of a real wealth portfolio rather than guilty indulgences. The thread running through every example is the same: Live the life you want now while building the life you want later. This is a fantastic book for taking control of your finances and, more importantly, for building a life your finances are designed to support."
—**Peter Laughter**, Keynote Speaker, "Collaborative Leadership in the Age of Disruption"

"I met Al Zdenek at a time when I was successful professionally but remarkably uninformed financially. Like many, I assumed that a physician's income automatically led to wealth. Al taught us that true wealth is not about income—it is about mastering cash flow, making disciplined financial choices, and creating freedom.

Today, I work because I want to, not because I need to. That simple distinction defines financial freedom. In this remarkable book and through the CakeClub app, Al and Amin offer readers the same opportunity I received decades ago: the knowledge, confidence, and tools to transform anxiety about money into clarity, control, and lasting wealth."
—**Hershey S. Bell, MD**, Dean, Methodist University Cape Fear Valley Health School of Medicine; Chief Academic Officer, Cape Fear Valley Health

"The most important financial lessons are rarely taught in school, and by the time most people realize that, the cost of not knowing them has already compounded. *Master Your Cash Flow* closes that gap with intelligence and generosity. Al Zdenek and Amin Boroomand have distilled decades of experiential wisdom into a framework that is both rigorous and deeply human, one that teaches readers to find money they didn't know they had, make decisions with clarity and confidence, and build toward financial freedom without sacrificing the life they want today. For the rising generation families I work with, this book arrives at exactly the right moment."

—**Lorna Gray**, Next Gen Leadership Expert; President & Founder, Interface Education Services LLC

MASTER YOUR CASH FLOW

Let Them Eat Cake And Build Wealth Too!

Albert J. Zdenek, Jr., CPA/PFS
Amin Boroomand, PhD

WEALTH AUTHORITY BOOKS

MASTER YOUR CASH FLOW

Let Them Eat Cake And Build Wealth Too!

Printed in the United States of America.

Paperback ISBN-13: 978-1-966168-85-0
Hardback ISBN-13: 978-1-966168-87-4
Library of Congress Control Number: 2026916864

Designed by Melissa Farr, Back Porch Creative, LLC

WEALTH AUTHORITY BOOKS
2511 WOODLANDS WAY
OCEANSIDE, CA 92054
www.indiebooksintl.com

Wealth Authority Books is an imprint of Indie Books International®, Inc.

To the intrepid who choose growth over comfort.

To the brave who take risks to constantly rewrite their story through learning and action.

To the courageous who leave home to build a better one.

Table Of Contents

Introduction

Let's Transform Your Life

By Al Zdenek

Some thirty years ago, on a dark and icy winter evening, I asked my wife, Margie, to have a seat in the living room of the beautiful Victorian house we had lovingly restored and shared with our two young sons. I could see the fear in her eyes. She knew we were on the verge of financial collapse, bankruptcy. Looking directly into those eyes, I softly said, "By the time we clean up the financial mess I have made, I am not sure we are going to be able to keep this house. We could lose everything." She cried. I was at the lowest point ever in my life.

I had founded many businesses and had been very successful at first. But poor managerial and cash-flow decisions slowly eroded this success. I had never been taught how to make good financial decisions. Now I needed help.

I was raised to think that asking for help was a weakness. I was ashamed and embarrassed. I was desperate. I finally reached out for advice and guidance. The generous and immediate help I received startled me.

One of those who helped was Daryl Cain, CPA, arguably one of the most successful financial planners at that time. The first thing he asked was about my cash-flow situation, what was coming in and going out. I didn't know. I just knew I didn't have enough to pay my bills. And I didn't know how to fix it.

He forced me to list and total my income and expenses. When I saw this laid out in front of me, I was even more depressed. How was I going to get this behind me? Would I be able to eventually live the lifestyle I wanted, travel, have a home or apartment, and hopefully have the choice to not have to work someday?

He saw my fear, frustration, and shame. I had an education. I should know this stuff.

"This is the trouble a lot of people get themselves into because they don't know how to make the best financial decisions for themselves, and effectively manage their cash flow," he gently said to me. He continued, "Now that you more clearly see your cash flow dilemma, let's get to work helping you clean it up."

I learned basic financial principles from him and learned how to make the best financial decisions for myself. I had no idea that I could determine when I could achieve financial freedom. I took steps over the next three to five years to not only clean up the mess I was in, but to recover, live the lifestyle I wanted, and set myself up for financial freedom in the time frame I wanted.

I was thirty-five years old. I eventually wanted to be financially free by fifty. With Daryl's coaching, I became a master of my cash flow. I achieved financial freedom by forty-eight.

If you've ever felt overwhelmed by money decisions nobody taught you how to make, you're not alone.

Amin Boroomand was a young PhD data scientist who, even after many years of education, couldn't figure out whether to lease or buy a car. He was shocked to realize that with all his education, he was unable more interest in your money than you.

To achieve what you want financially, you may have ... spending plan (some call this a budget, but we don't like that word and will cover "creating a spending plan" later in the book) or some beginnings of a financial plan. This book will help you with these actions and provide you with a "roadmap" to guide you to:

- make better financial choices
- reduce any personal-finance-related fear, frustration, or stress you may have in your life
- help you to see how you could achieve financial freedom in the years you want or perhaps in three-to-five-year time frames (short-term financial goals), if this suits you more

...they wanted both now and along the way to ... financial freedom. He wanted to pay it forward.

On a picture-perfect fall day, October 23, 2023, he sat down for lunch with me at Cafe Fiorello in NYC. By the end of that lunch, CakeClub Inc., his vision for the CakeClub app, was born.

Our lives were changed when we learned how to make better financial decisions and how to master cash flow. Now we want to help you.

We founded CakeClub to create a personal finance app with the philosophy that you do not have to punish and deprive yourself of the spending pleasures you want in life if you learn how to consistently make the best financial decisions and focus on finding and saving cash flow. You will experience less stress around money, achieve financial freedom sooner, see how you are able to work fewer years, and live the lifestyle you wish along the way.

to make the most basic financial decisions. He saw his colleagues and friends in the same bind.

He began to question if he would be able to live the lifestyle he wanted or even afford to have a family. Stressed and fearful, he was frustrated, not knowing how to make the best financial decisions or even where to begin to learn. It was overwhelming.

He started to read articles I had written over the years and my books, *Master Your Cash Flow: The Key to Grow And Retain Wealth* (ForbesBooks, 2017) and *Master Your Business Cash Flow: Grow the Company You Love, Live the Life You Want Now* (ForbesBooks, 2018).

The books resonated with him. He could now clearly see how to make better financial decisions, become a master of his cash flow, live the lifestyle he wanted, and achieve financial freedom when he wanted.

Amin had a vision. Having fintech talent and experience, he wanted to change the world. He wanted to make financial education accessible to everyone. He wanted everyone to make the best financial decisions and to live the lifestyl

achievin

This is the mission of CakeClub. This is what you will start to learn in this book.

So, let's play a game together. This game is called "Master Your Cash Flow." Of course, when starting a new game and wanting the best chance to win, it is good to know the rules of the game.

The Ground Rules For Success

To win or receive the maximum benefit out of this book, let's start with the ground rules for success.

Rule 1: This Book May Not Answer All Of Your Questions, But It's A Great Start

This book is meant to answer as many of your questions as possible, reduce frustration and stress you might have, and allow you to think of more questions.

It's meant to educate and guide you. You may see recommendations, but ultimately, you make all the decisions. No one is going to do this for you. This is your life; this is your money. No one is going to have

to create a

- help you understand, if you have accumulated some savings or wealth, how to preserve this wealth while continuing to build new wealth

Your spending plan, some financial goals, or the beginnings of a financial plan will serve as your action plan toward achieving initial and maybe longer-term goals. These will serve as a guidepost for you to monitor your progress monthly or annually, ensuring you are on the right track to achieving your financial goals.

Rule 2: This Is Your Financial Life And You Must Participate In It

Yes, this book will provide education and awareness, but you will eventually need others, what we call an "expert team" to accomplish what you want. We will get more into this later in the book but remember, no matter how good your accountant, attorney, investment, or other adviser is, they cannot make decisions for you. Financial choices are your choices, not theirs. Your choices will eventually determine how you live, now and in the future. Don't hand the reins to just anyone.

Your Wealth Building Formula and roadmap (later explained) will serve as guides on your financial journey. Keep in mind, while your journey may go slowly at first, this is a marathon, not a sprint. Pay attention, ask questions of your experts, and take an active role or you may not achieve what you want.

Rule 3: Past Decisions—Let Them Go

You may have made some good financial moves and some disastrous ones. You might feel regret, embarrassment, or have some trust issues over the bad ones. Don't focus on them. This book is here to help you make better financial choices going *forward* that are aligned with your financial and lifestyle goals.

Rule 4: What You Can Expect From This Book

The goals of this book are to answer many of the questions you may have, with clarity, to give you a process for making better financial choices, to educate you in financial principles and concepts, such as making the best cash flow management decisions, and inspire you to commit to and achieve the financial goals that allow you to live the life you want now and in the future.

Let's get started.

1

Making Better Financial Choices

Determining How You Wish To Live Your Life

The boomers are all about money.
Gen X is like, "Is it all about money?"
Millennials are like, "Where is the money?"
And Gen Z is like, "What is money?"
—Amy Poehler, comedian and actor

How do people in their twenties and thirties make financial choices? Often, they don't do so as well as they need to, largely because they're poorly informed about the impact of the choices they're making. It's not their fault; sadly, financial education in our country is nearly nonexistent. You're typically not taught enough personal finance in high school or college. You're taught history, math, and languages, but there's usually no course in which it's mandatory for you to understand how to balance your checkbook, how to apply for a car loan or a credit card, or how to save money, much less how to plan to buy a home.

A young software engineer once asked us what a CD was. He sheepishly said that he'd heard about these things that banks offered, but he didn't know what they were. This is a man who was successful and well-trained within his field, but somehow his extensive education hadn't included an explanation of what a certificate of deposit was.

Typically, when people go into their first job, their employer asks them if they want to participate in the company's 401(k). The new hire nods but is most likely thinking, "What is a 401(k)?" or "Why do I need it?" They have no idea what a 401(k) is versus an IRA (individual retirement account).

Added to that is the fact that, as a consumer-oriented society, we're drilled with the idea that, "OK, you've just gone through four years of study to get a college education. You deserve a really nice car and a wallet full of credit cards." Young (and some not-so-young) people make the mistake of taking on a lot of debt when they're least able to handle it.

If this is you, you are not alone. We work with some of the smartest people around—young entrepreneurs, attorneys, CPAs, business owners, and those climbing the ladder of major corporations—and they all have this same problem. They become masters at what they do, whether that's working at a medical practice, an accounting firm, a law firm, their own business, or a major corporation, but when it comes to their personal financial lives, they haven't the faintest idea how to manage their personal cash flow.

A manager once told coauthor Al, "I just got back from seeing my tax accountant. She told me that I earned almost $150,000 last year. I was stunned. I asked her, 'Where did it all go?'" Yes, this manager was a master at managing, but she's not a master of her cash flow.

The fact is, if you want to create the life that you want now and in the future, you have to become the master of your cash flow—you need to understand some basics of finance and to learn to make better financial choices.

You're Not Necessarily Bad With Money. You're Playing A Harder Game.

If any of these sound familiar, you're not alone:

- "I'm scared to open my bank app."
- "I don't know where my money went."
- "I feel guilty every time I spend."
- "I make money but feel broke."
- "I'm embarrassed I'm bad with money."

Let's say the quiet part out loud: Money got harder.

In the last few decades, the *same* basic milestones have become more expensive and more complex.

Housing costs hit record highs, and the inflation-adjusted monthly payment on a median-priced home is roughly 40 percent higher than in 1990. Meanwhile, the national home price-to-income ratio has climbed to record territory. In the 1990s, a typical home cost about 3.2 times the median household income. In 2024, it cost about 5 times that income.[1] Since 1990, national rents have increased about 226 percent, while real median household income has increased only about 28 percent.[2]

Education costs are equally staggering: Federal student loan debt has surpassed $1.7 trillion, with about 43 million Americans carrying federal student loans. Meanwhile, inflation-adjusted tuition and fees at public four-year institutions have roughly doubled since the mid-1990s.[3] Public four-year college tuition (after inflation) rose from about $5,740 in the mid-1990s to about $11,610 today. Private four-year college tuition rose from about $24,840 to about $43,350 (after inflation).[4]

The average credit card interest rate is about 22 percent, one of the highest levels in modern history.[5]

So if your brain treats money like a threat, that's not weakness. That's pattern recognition.

Here's the twist: You still have leverage. And it starts with one uncomfortable truth: Your "money problem" is often an "avoidance problem."

Not because you're irresponsible, but because uncertainty is stressful, and your brain tries to protect you by not looking.

— Application Box —
Amin's Mirror Move (60 Seconds)

Do this once a day for one week:

1. Open your money dashboard (bank app, spreadsheet, whatever you use).
2. Look at two numbers only:
   - What's available right now
   - What's leaving next (upcoming bills/charges)
3. Close it.

That's it. No spreadsheets. No guilt. No spiral.

You're building tolerance for reality, the same way you build strength at the gym: small reps, consistently.

Because clarity doesn't restrict you. Clarity *frees you.*

When you can see what's true, you stop guessing. And when you stop guessing, you stop leaking confidence (and cash) in the dark.

If you want it easier, use a tool that pulls everything into one place, connects accounts and cards, or lets you add transactions manually, so the truth becomes simple enough to face. The goal isn't perfection. The goal is not to be surprised by your own life.

And yes, your savior is in the mirror.

It's you, finally looking.

How Do You Make A Better Financial Choice?

The answer to that question begins with another question: What kind of lifestyle do you wish to live *now*? There is a certain amount of cash flow that, if you had it coming in right now and for the rest of your life, inflation-adjusted, would allow you to live the lifestyle you want now and make you financially independent. Discovering that number is the first thing on which to focus. This will help you determine how much wealth you might want to accumulate over the next three to five years or longer.

There are a lot of "experts" who will tell you that you can figure this out on your own—maybe just by reading their book, taking a course, or putting your numbers in a software program. While figures can be calculated, the choices you make to accumulate wealth or to preserve and manage it are much more complex so make sure you choose an expert, or even an app that will educate you as well as guide you.

For example, we know one person who just joined an organization whose members explored how to invest and review investment opportunities every month. After eight months of meetings, she told us, "I have learned so much. I now know how I want to invest my money." While we are sure she learned a good deal more about investing than she had previously known, investment management isn't that simple. It is a complex chore.

Like investing, the effect of financial choices regarding cash flow, debt, taxes, insurance, estate planning, investing, and other financial aspects of one's life is much more complicated than one typically imagines. Making the wrong choices can ensure that you work longer in life, you don't live the lifestyle you want because you are left with less wealth and cash flow, or the risk in your investment portfolio is increased.

It's natural for people who are masters in their own professions or businesses to assume that they can easily master the complexities of portfolio investment. They think that they can read a book, read the financial pages, follow a TV show, and more or less "visit" their money once every month or three and become as expert at managing it as people who do this as their profession, 24-7. How realistic is this?

Let's say that you wanted to master the game of tennis. If you play tennis one day a year, we doubt that you'd play very well. Maybe you think to yourself, *I'd improve if I played tennis once a month.* You might progress a little bit, but probably not a lot. But you're determined to master this, so you decide to play tennis three times a week. Granted, you're probably never going to be Novak Djokovic or Serena Williams, but you know what? You'll play tennis a lot better with that constant practice than you would have if you did it once a year or once a month. So, being involved in decisions around your money is important to "play" better and better recognize what help you might need.

So, could you do better if you became more involved with your portfolio? Sure. But as Benjamin Graham, Warren Buffett's mentor and the author of the iconic book *The Intelligent Investor*, suggested, achieving good returns is not hard if you are willing to spend the time, but achieving superior returns is harder than it looks.[6] It is tough to do unless you are doing this 24-7. Again, search out experts who do this work 24-7, but also remain involved.

Yet this is exactly what people do regarding their finances; a lot of very bright people get medical degrees, law degrees, accounting degrees, or financial degrees or establish successful companies, and because they're experts in their respective arenas, they assume that they can "visit" the investment management area or other areas of finance and know all there is to know about it.

Al once jokingly asked a surgeon, "Can I take a course for a few days, read a book, or watch a series on TV, and then go and do heart surgery?" This might be a good start, but you need to respect the fact that there are people who do their kind of work all day, every day, and are masters at it, whether it's in insurance, banking, accounting, estate work, or investment portfolio management. You cannot become an expert in all these areas, but you can surround yourself with experts who are equipped to help educate and guide you to make better financial choices.

Al has given many lectures before groups of graduates who have just finished college, and to other young professionals and executives just starting out their careers. He often starts his speeches this way: "I see you when you become more serious about money in about twenty years, when you've really screwed up or you've made bad financial choices around debt, investments, or other financial matters. You're in your forties or fifties, and suddenly sixty doesn't look that far away, and now you're scared. Then you come to wealth experts like me so that you can start to set things right."

Al and Amin want to help you today to learn how to avoid some or all of those mistakes. That way, while you still may need some help, you are going to be in better financial shape in ten, twenty, or thirty years.

But it's important to understand that making better financial choices is not something you can visit once in a while or learn to do simply by watching FinTok videos, reading a book (even this one), or by taking a course. While a great start, again, your best bet is to surround yourself with people who will help guide you in making better financial choices through a financial plan that lays out how you want to live now and in the future.

Do you want less stress, frustration, and anxiety? Do you want more clarity concerning your current spending and how much you have to save? Is the plan you have now, plus what you're going to add to it, going to be enough? What is the average annual rate of return you need from your investment portfolio that makes everything work (what we call your long-term investment return objective)? Is your wealth protected?

Do you have a tax accountant? Or do you just rely on an online product like TurboTax? If you do have an accountant, is she calling you up before the end of the year to work up a tax projection of what your year looks like? She had better be because once the calendar year ends, nothing can be done. Or does your accountant just call you up on April 14 to inform you that you owe a lot of money . . . tomorrow? Possibly you didn't get your information into your accountant until February, March, or April. You were too busy, and she is used to you being late anyway, and just views your situation as tax work. In this case, your accountant is not helping you make better financial choices, find more cash flow, or build a financial future.

Even If You Already Have Accumulated Some Wealth, You Need To Know How Money Works

There was a great article in *The New York Times*: "The Bad Fortune of Some Ultrawealthy People."[7] Just because you are well-off or rich doesn't mean you can't lose your wealth. If you're one of those very fortunate people who have the wealth to live the way you want now, it's important to make sure you can preserve and manage that wealth so that, in the future, you don't lose it because of poor financial decisions. You may be living a great lifestyle, but you wonder if you can sustain it or improve upon it.

We work with people of all income ranges; one example is a young couple Al met who had accumulated a few rental properties from which they were getting dependable rental income cash flow. They lived pretty simple lives and weren't outlandish in their spending. But there was an unanticipated change in the economy in their area, and all of a sudden they experienced some vacancies, which meant that their cash flow suddenly shrank.

Even though they owned their real estate free and clear, without debt, instead of it having positive cash flow, they were now paying for their holdings out of pocket. Why? They still had to pay for maintenance, real estate taxes, and other operational expenses, all of which cut deeply into their income and jeopardized their savings.

to produce the cash flow they expected. They got what they wished and secured that cash flow for the rest of their lives.

Another example of how you can fix broken cash flow even later in the game was a client of Al's who was a former senior executive of a Fortune 500 company who retired in his forties and was now in his fifties. He was badly hit in a stock market crash because the investment holdings in his portfolio weren't sufficiently diversified. He had always had adequate cash flow before, so he and his wife had never really paid that much attention to their portfolio. Now they had to because their wealth was down quite a lot and was greatly affecting their cash flow.

Mind you, these are people who had a beautiful apartment, were active in charities, and were used to traveling every year. Now they were on what we call a "survivor budget." They had pared down their life so much that they could not support the charities anymore. They scrapped

you were in debt when you retired, you had to
something. When the market changed, they weren't getting
same cash flow out of their properties. If they approached a bank to get a loan to cover some of the shortfall, what was the bank likely to do? A bank is only going to be your friend in good times; a bank is not there to take on risk and will only give you loans if you have adequate cash flow. Banks only give you money when you don't need them. This couple couldn't get loans from banks because even though they had the assets, they did not have the cash flow. They'd put all their eggs in on basket—and then dropped the basket.

What were we able to do? We looked at what they had and what th
have to do with their properties to get themselves out of this situa
There was one property they owned that, even in good times, w
good cash flow producer, but they'd held on to it for personal re

Not surprisingly, at that point, they panicked; they made some bad choices and got behind on their real estate taxes. Suddenly, they were looking at a scenario in which they'd be forced to sell their properties in a down market, which would put them into a downward financial spiral of less and less income. They were trapped and didn't know which way to turn. That was the point at which they sought us out.

How Can You Fix Broken Cash Flow?

What poor financial choices had this couple made that brought them to this point? Certainly, somewhere along the line, they could have ensured they had significant cash reserves or diversified into asset classes other than real estate. They could have sold off some of that real estate when the market was high and gotten into those other investments so that when that got hit, they would not be so badly affected.

Another mistake was one that most people make: They wanted to be out of debt as soon as possible. To them, having no debt was a sign of being successful. If

have failed

the

That kind of thinking isn't helpful when you're trying to build cash flow. Bad real estate is like a bad stock. When the market goes down, if you're in a bad stock, you'd better sell it. If you're in a good stock, you can hold onto it because good stocks normally come back, just as good real estate normally comes back. Bad real estate and bad stocks do not, so there was some real estate they had to let go.

When they did that, their cash flow improved because they were not stuck throwing money at this bad property. When their cash flow improved, we were able to go to a bank and show the bank that they were taking steps to improve cash flow. The bank decided that now they were a better risk, so it gave them some short-term borrowing ability. The borrowing allowed them to fix up properties to attract better tenants and to pay their expenses, so they didn't lose the other two properties.

Then, as the market improved, they were able to take some of the excess cash flow and finally diversify into other assets. Even though it took a few years and they weren't able to keep all their property, the property and investments they had left were good, and they were able [illegible] they required [illegible] to live the lifestyle they [illegible] their annual trip. Their apartment accrued deferred maintenance because they couldn't afford to fix it.

As with many people who don't plan their finances properly or make poor financial choices, cash flow can seem to be all right in early retirement years, but can suddenly become tight later—and it was becoming very tight for this couple. He was scared because his wife was younger, her mother was still alive, and his wife could easily live much longer. He was concerned about what to do.

Al looked at his cash flow calculation very carefully and said, "I think you've made a mistake. I think you're a little short on your cash flow."

Scared, the client asked Al, "What do you mean?"

Al said, "Well, don't you want to live the way you did before? Don't you want to travel to Europe? Don't you want to participate again in your charities? Don't you want to fix up this apartment and make sure, at the same time, your wife is going to be able to be financially independent beyond your own passing?"

He looked at Al and said, "If you could do that, that would be incredible."

We looked at how he was structured around his taxes, his portfolio, and his debt, and we brought some better financial choices to what he was doing. With better choices, we were able to return him to the cash flow that allowed him to live the lifestyle he wanted to, but also assured that his wife could continue to live in that same fashion, even if she lived to be one hundred.

It is nearly never too late to correct poor choices to improve one's cash flow and financial condition. Doing so for this couple transformed their lives.

Don't Set Out Without A Map

You might be thinking, "These problems of the wealthy don't apply to me." This isn't about being wealthy; it is about avoiding financial problems. Of course, it's a lot easier to solve financial problems before they happen.

It's analogous to taking a road trip. If you decide, "I'm in New York City, and I want to go to San Francisco," you can immediately walk out of your home, get into your car without any planning and just start traveling west on the highways that seem to be going in that direction—and hopefully, you'll get there somewhat in the time frame you wanted.

Alternatively, you could map your route on your phone, research the trip online, or consult a travel agent and plan your trip, including where to stop overnight, so that you know where you are at all times, can check your progress daily, and arrive at the time you wish and in the condition you desire.

A good financial strategy is like that; it lets you say, "There's a goal I have in mind, but there's a preferred route I'd like to travel along on the way toward that goal—one that guarantees I'll get there in the manner I wish and be safe en route." If you can do that, it greatly decreases the stress and anxiety you'll experience along the way.

When life throws surprises at you, you'll be better able to handle them. Have you ever started out on a road trip only to discover that one of the major interstates is closed by an accident? If you have a good map, you can quickly find an alternate route.

That's all this is. Sometimes people make seemingly random choices or quick decisions because they're busy and want to get it out of the way, but they'll put the time into planning a vacation, for instance, because that's more immediately enjoyable. That's the difference between someone making good financial choices and someone who sets themself up for potentially making bad financial choices.

Being young can be a great advantage. The younger you are when you start, the more time is on your side.

— Application Box —

Amin's $500 Freedom Buffer

Most financial stress isn't caused by huge disasters. It's caused by small surprises at the worst time: a flat tire, an unexpected deductible, a broken laptop charger that ruins a whole day.

The Federal Reserve has tracked this for years: A meaningful share of adults still can't cover a $400 surprise with cash (or its equivalent).[8]

So here's the move: Before you chase big investing goals, build a small buffer.

Rule: Your first win is $500 set aside.

Not for vacations. Not for shopping. For "life happened."

How:

- Set an automatic transfer of $10–$25 after every paycheck.
- Put it into a separate account labeled Freedom Buffer.
- Stop at $500.

This isn't about the amount. It's about buying options for yourself—the ability to begin to handle life with some freedom.

What We Don't Know Can Hurt Us

It comes down to how people are taught to make financial choices. We're usually taught in a few ways, but our first teachers are likely to be our parents. When we're first out into the adult world and need advice, we might ask Mom or Dad, "How did you handle that?" We may start doing the same things our parents did.

We may ask an older brother, sister, or friend; listen to influencers or podcasts; or read articles. We don't stop to think that the content is generalized enough to apply to the masses; somehow we think that it's customized to us, but it is not.

Ultimately, we may make our choices the way others tell us to, or based on how we've seen them make their choices. We don't judge whether they've been good or bad at it.

We wouldn't do this in other spheres: When you're really ill, you don't listen to a podcast; you go to a doctor and put your trust into their hands to guide you past that illness.

Unfortunately, perhaps, poor financial "health" doesn't always alert us with recognizable symptoms in the way that poor physical health usually does; often, the effects of our poor financial choices creep up on us over a longer period. We don't see the financial illness show up for ten, twenty, thirty, or forty years, until finally we're much older. Now, cash flow is getting tight, and we can't afford certain things because we didn't realize that the decisions we made long ago would affect us in the ways they do today.

If someone were on fire, their response would be immediate: They would jump up and down and scream in pain, right? When financial professionals like us see you making poor financial choices, it is like seeing you on fire, except you are not jumping up and down and screaming. You are just sitting there, burning, maybe even pouring on more gas by making more poor financial choices.

When it's a "financial fire," people often don't feel the burn right away, so they just keep on going as they have been. If you have an infected appendix and choose not to have it removed, you're going to feel it pretty quickly. If you make a poor financial decision, you may not realize it for many years. You need a good financial "physician" to guide you.

Options Equal Financial Freedom

People want options, like the option of going to work or not. Most head off to work every day as though on a treadmill. Statistics tell us that a lot of people don't really enjoy the work they do, but they do it because they have to survive, because they have to feed the family, or because they feel caught.[9]

A lot of people do their job because that's what their mother or father did or what they were told to do in pursuit of success. That job is not necessarily something that they love. But whether or not people love their job, as they're earning money, they want to know that somewhere along the way, they will have options.

Ava graduated with a degree in marketing. She interned for a while, but it did not develop into the full-time job she expected. Undeterred, she got a position in retail at a department store, but not earning enough, she worked part-time as a barista at Starbucks. It was discouraging for her, but finally, after two seemingly unending years, she landed a job at a high-end marketing shop, working on exclusive fashion labels.

Her dream job, though, was to have her own marketing firm. While she worked full-time with her employer, she plotted her escape: She started to consult start-ups on marketing their products in her spare time. While it took another four years of building a contact network and enough clientele to leave her full-time position, she finally opened her own marketing firm.

She created a plan that eventually gave her the option to work for herself and determine how she wanted to live and work.

Liam graduated a few years ago with a high GPA and a business degree. The problem is when he graduated, no one was hiring. He finally found a job at an accounting firm as a receptionist. While feeling lucky to have a job, as many of his friends did not, this was certainly not the career he was looking for. In fact, he was not sure of what he really wanted to do as a career. But he did know he wanted to stop having to depend on his parents for help paying the rent on his place.

Then, he suddenly had the opportunity to help with small details with the accountants and clients. From a mentor, he discovered that the company would pay for courses in accounting and tax. Taking some courses, and working with clients, he found that he enjoyed the work. He eventually secured a position as an accountant at his company, but his dream became to work for himself.

His mentor, a much older accountant, helped guide him, and along with his financial courses, reading, and listening to podcasts, he learned how to make better financial decisions. Since he now could prepare tax returns, he did this work and some bookkeeping for small companies on the side as he worked full-time.

It did not happen overnight, but Liam eventually joined forces with another accountant and opened up their own accounting office.

While he didn't have a plan at first, he eventually had a dream, a vision of how he wanted to work and live his life. He learned how to improve his skills, learned how to make better financial decisions, and, by working side gigs, developed the option to open his own business.

If people know that making better financial decisions will eventually give them more options in life, that lights them up. It can transform their lives. They can see that they can eventually work at careers they want—to go out and contribute to society or to live in a way they'd never thought they could.

For Al, realizing that he could have these options was a turning point for him. For the first time in his life, he saw that it was in his power to make choices that would ensure, by age fifty or sooner, that when he went to work, he would be there because he wanted to be, not because he had to be.

Just close your eyes and imagine the feeling that comes with that certainty; suddenly, there's no stress or anxiety, and we think that's what a lot of people want. They want to know that there are options in their life, that they can continue to work, if that's their preference, or do something else, take more risks, and decide who they want to deal with or not in their life.

Making better financial choices can mean that you have those options sooner rather than later—or even that you have them at all. What keeps people from making those choices properly are what we call "the obstacles," which we'll talk about in the next chapter.

The "Money Intake Form"

A friend once told coauthor Amin they had a stress-scrolling problem. Not "I check my phone" scrolling. The *2:00 a.m., suddenly I'm watching a stranger restore a rusty knife* kind.

When the friend shared their problem with their therapist, she didn't start with a pep talk. She started with a question: "What triggers it?"

Not to judge it. To *map* it. Because once you can name the pattern, you can change the pattern.

Money works the same way.

If you work hard but your savings never look the way you want, don't begin with shame. Begin with a metaphorical "intake form." Before trying to fix your money, first gather the basic facts, the way a physician or therapist starts by understanding what is going on.

- How much do you make each month?
- How much do you spend each month?
- Where is it going by category?
- What are your fixed bills?
- What patterns or triggers drive extra spending?

If you can't answer a few basic questions, you're not necessarily "bad with money." You're just flying without instruments.

— Application Box —
Amin's Three-Number Reality Check

1. How much money hits your account each month (after taxes)?
2. How much leaves your account in fixed spending or bills that have to be paid?
3. How much leaves your account for flexible spending, and where does it go? (Food, shopping, rides, subscriptions, etc.)

Most people *want* to manage spending, but tracking and budgeting often feel overwhelming—and even many people with a budget don't benchmark against it regularly. That's why the Consumer Financial Protection Bureau found that over 90 percent of the people they interviewed were interested in real-time spending feedback tools and expected those tools to curb impulse spending and reduce uncertainty.[10]

Translation: You're not alone for avoiding the numbers. Avoidance is a normal response to stress. But it's an expensive coping skill.

How To Get The Numbers (Without Making It A Whole Personality)

You can do with pen and paper, a spreadsheet, or an app. The tool doesn't matter. The visibility does.

If you want the easiest visibility path, use a personal finance app that pulls everything into one place. Look for one that connects to your bank accounts and credit cards, or lets you enter transactions manually, and categorizes spending so the pattern is obvious.

If using pen, paper, and a spreadsheet, answer the following questions:

- How much money hits your account each month (after taxes)?
- How much leaves your account for fixed, non-negotiable expenses? (Rent, utilities, insurance, minimum payments).
- How much do you spend on flexible categories each month, and where does it go? (Food, shopping, transport, subscriptions, etc.).
- What subscriptions or recurring charges are you paying for right now?
- What debts do you have, and what are their interest rates and minimum payments?
- How much do you currently have in savings, and how many months of expenses does it cover?
- When and why do you tend to overspend? (Patterns, triggers, situations).
- How are you currently tracking or reviewing your money? (If at all).
- What is your primary financial goal for the next twelve months?

The Trigger Map (The Part Nobody Does)

Once you have the numbers, ask yourself one more question: When does spending become "automatic"?

Common triggers look like the following.

- Time: late-night purchases, weekend "treat myself" spirals
- Mood: stress, boredom, loneliness, celebration
- People: group plans, weddings, "everyone's doing it" energy
- Place: the checkout line, airport, Target runs that become a hobby

You're not trying to eliminate temptation. You're trying to stop being surprised by it.

CakeClub Slices

- You are not necessarily bad with money.
- Begin by calculating, in dollars, the total cost per year of the life you wish to live.
- Don't set out on your financial journey without a roadmap (provided in the next chapter).
- Options mean financial freedom.
- Address the "money intake form" and the "three-number reality check."

2

The Obstacles

I'm gonna quit my job and travel the world
until I run out of money!
I estimate I'll be home again around 10 p.m. this evening.
—Taylor Tomlinson, comedian

Obstacles are thoughts or ideas that people have about finance that prevent them from making better financial choices, which in turn prevent them from living life the way they wish now, achieving short-term goals, and becoming financially independent when they want, or, if they are already independent, from maintaining that independence and continuing to grow their wealth.

Growing wealth is an obstacle for many. Studies show that most Americans lag in even building emergency savings. A 2025 survey conducted by Talker Research examined Gen Z's financial health and how money difficulties have affected their overall well-being, work, and retirement plans.

According to the findings, most Gen Z members (77 percent) think they'll need to work past the typical retirement age to make ends meet:

Half (49 percent) believe they'll need to work full-time, and 29 percent anticipate they'll need to work at least part-time.

And while, on the whole, 67 percent of Gen Z hourly workers are still proactively saving for retirement, less than half of those who don't think they'll retire are still saving for it just in case (44 percent), putting this significant group of people in a precarious financial position.[11]

There are really two categories of obstacles: *practical* and *emotional.*

The Practical Obstacles

There are four practical obstacles:

- *No* specific goals in dollar terms
- *No* written document
- *No* process to achieve goals
- *No* roadmap

The first practical obstacle is a lack of specific goals with attached amounts of money. The most common contributor to this is that while most people have an idea of how they would like to live now or in the future, they have no idea what that lifestyle will actually cost them in dollars.

Emma worked as an administrative assistant in a law firm. She had dreams of possibly going to law school, but in the moment what she wanted was to be able to afford an apartment for herself. She shared an apartment with two friends, and while they got along, it was not as private as she wanted.

She had a conversation with us. We asked her, "How much would you have to earn annually to afford an apartment, pay your current school loans, and pay your other expenses and income taxes?"

"I don't know," she responded.

We then had her list and total all of her expenses, including making sure she could take a vacation, have dinners with friends, attend concerts, and continue to enjoy her daily lattes. The total came to about double what she was earning now. She was shocked and depressed, thinking, *How am I ever going to live the way I want?*

We then asked her when the last time was that she discussed her future with her employer. What could her compensation be in the future?

She did and found out they would not be able to pay her what she needed to get her apartment and live the way she wanted. Emma started to look at other employers. She found a law firm that allowed her to work as a legal assistant and give her an opportunity to earn more. She took the job.

While it was still not enough income to cover 100 percent of what she needed, it was close. She decided to work part-time at home as an administrative assistant to small firms in her spare time. She got her apartment.

In a couple of years, she didn't need the side gigs to afford her lifestyle anymore, but she kept a few she enjoyed. Last time we talked to her, she was thinking of a career as a COO (chief operating officer) for a law firm.

Emma did not know how much she needed to live the way she wanted. We showed her that all that was required to get by this "obstacle" was to calculate what she needed. Once someone knows what they need, they can start to plan or make decisions that will allow them to achieve what they want.

People who define their goals and clarity in dollars will know where they stand and have the choice to make good financial decisions.

The second practical obstacle is that people have no written plan for achieving their goals. Since there's nothing in writing, there's really no point of reference that they can look back at a year or two years from now to see if they're on the right track or how to correct their course of action.

The third practical obstacle is that people don't have a process—a way of making decisions or taking actions that gets them there from here.

Take, as an example, a person who says, "I want to be vice president of the company rather than a manager." How do they achieve it? What's required in terms of training? What's the process to moving up?

The last obstacle is that people have no roadmap. Again, if you're on a trip from New York to San Francisco, you can just get on the road and know that it's west somewhere, or you can take out a roadmap. That map is going to make you more efficient and more effective.

People often have no financial roadmap. With the amount of savings they have, no matter what it is, they have no idea if they're a quarter of the way, a third of the way, or halfway to what they need to achieve. Sometimes they don't even know if they have reached their goal.

These four practical obstacles can keep people from living the life they wish now and in the future, from achieving financial freedom or independence in the time frame they wish, and from staying financially independent.

What Would Apple Do?

Companies must also navigate these four practical obstacles, and how a well-run company manages them often provides a good example for how individuals can approach them.

A well-run company like Apple, for instance, has well-defined goals. Its leaders know what profit they're aiming for this year. They know the earnings per share, return on equity, and other benchmarks they have to achieve. Their goals are clear and defined in absolute numbers and percentages.

Al worked for Merck & Co. Inc., where even his department—the corporate tax department—had well-defined financial goals. They had budgets. As a department, they reviewed their numbers monthly and quarterly, not just at the end of the year.

A good financial plan will have well-defined goals and numbers attached to it.

The second practical obstacle is having nothing in writing. Everything in a well-run company is written; monthly and quarterly budgets are planned a year in advance, perhaps even years in advance.

But typically, individuals don't plan in writing that far ahead with their personal finances, and that's a problem. If you don't have well-defined written goals in absolute dollar figures and/or percentages, you cannot know if you achieved your goals nor can you make appropriate adjustments during the year if you get behind.

The third practical obstacle is having no process. A well-run company has good training. From day one, you know what your job is. You know the systems of the company, and if you don't, they offer superior training programs.

Individuals often do not know the steps to accomplish what they need; their "training" in personal finance is usually haphazard at best and is often achieved on the fly.

Finally, the fourth obstacle is the lack of a roadmap. Well-run companies don't have that problem; they know where they are throughout the year. This is why companies hire more people, lay people off, or sell divisions in the middle of a year. They don't wait until the end of the year and say, "Gee, I wonder what I did last year?" They take actions throughout the year to ensure they meet their goals.

A good short-term or long-term financial plan will include each of the following:

- Goals in specific dollar terms
- A written document (a plan)
- Processes to achieve goals
- A roadmap

With anything less, you have a much poorer chance of achieving what you want now and in the future. Be an Apple.

The Emotional Obstacles

The emotional obstacles are feelings and beliefs that can prevent people from living the life they wish or achieving and maintaining financial freedom, even if they are progressing past the practical obstacles.

We find that the biggest emotion that stops people from doing things is fear. Fear of what?

One common situation is that people have had a painful prior experience with a decision involving money and are fearful of making the same mistake again. For example, almost all of us have seen the stock markets correct or crash. If we made a bad investment decision, or the markets crashed and we lost money, we're scared to invest because we're worried that we will lose money again. This wariness could prevent some from taking even measured risks, effectively paralyzing them.

Another fear is lack of knowledge. People with high school and college degrees and career success think they should already know this financial stuff. Sometimes they're embarrassed to be sitting with people like us and having to admit they don't know what certain financial terms mean.

To get beyond that, you have to admit to yourself that you don't know something and then go out and find the answer, rather than ignoring it or being ashamed.

Then there are the people who think that they already know everything. Ever know someone like that? It often seems like you can't help them; you couldn't possibly add to their knowledge, because they read a book and think they're experts. That's another emotional obstacle: thinking that you already know everything and not really admitting or understanding that actually you may not.

What are other kinds of fears? There are fears about how others might view you. That can be tied to your faith or simply to how you were raised. People sometimes fear that if they have wealth, others might think they're morally corrupt and that their gains must somehow be ill-gotten. There's so much emotion around money that we get confused about it as a society. Sometimes we feel guilty if we have done very well in our lives compared to our families and friends, so we don't like to talk about it. That too can lead to poor financial choices.

Trust is a big obstacle. If you've been burned by a friend, relative, or an adviser—accountant, attorney, investment adviser, or insurance agent—you may have problems trusting someone else.

Another obstacle is cost: Good advice comes at a cost, and some people don't want to pay for it, so they will hunt for something that costs less or do it themselves. Influencers play on these emotions. They might say, "You don't have to pay anything. Just listen to a podcast. Just watch a program. You can make your own smart financial decisions." Some financial salespeople say, "Your planning is free or included in the cost to manage your investments." You have heard that "there is no such thing as a free lunch." There is a cost for everything. People are so afraid of getting burned by paying a fee that they fall for these ploys—and into making ruinous choices.

A good wealth adviser or financial planner is going to be able to help you with your practical obstacles, and a good adviser also will listen to your emotional obstacles and help you to work through them. Some people may never wholly free themselves from emotional obstacles; they can, however, learn how to recognize and handle them.

How do you handle fear? If you remember the first time you had to speak before your class or a large audience, you may have been scared; but most likely, you got by it. You handled it. If you have kids, maybe when you held your first child, the thought in your mind was, *What am I going to do?* But you got through it.

You start handling things because that's the only way to progress. You may never lose the fear, but you learn to deal with it. It's exactly the same way with emotional obstacles. You just handle them.

Don't Let Your Emotional Obstacles Dictate Your Future

Everyone has emotional obstacles of one kind or another. Don't let them create a greater obstacle—one that prevents you from living the life you want, now and in the future. Don't let them dictate your financial choices and do you harm. Face them, and take control once and for all.

Finance is not all about figures. Helping a person live the life they want and putting together a financial plan for them is not all about numbers. We can make a person or a couple financially independent remarkably quickly. All we have to do is tell a young person or couple, "Don't have kids and don't buy a house; live in a shack, don't go out to movies or take vacations, eat instant ramen every day, and we'll get you there fast."

But living the life you want means being satisfied with the way in which you live now. We can get you there quickly using the advice laid out in our example above, but then you and your significant other may not be talking to each other in ten years.

Financial choices are also balanced with personal choices. This is why one of the ground rules for us is that we educate you. We'll guide and recommend, but you make all the financial decisions because financial decisions have to be made around what is important to you in life.

Oliver, a twenty-five-year-old young entrepreneur and mentee of Al, called in one day.

He told Al, "I have goals I want to achieve by the time I reach thirty, and I don't think having a relationship or marriage is in the cards for me. Yeah, I want kids someday, but I just don't feel that I can have a family and achieve what I want."

Al listened and explained that he sounded like he was stuck in "seesaw" thinking. You've seen seesaws in children's playgrounds. A seesaw works where one side goes up, and the other side goes down, one choice or the other. People think like this too: "If I want to be able to save and live the life I want, I can't have a family or travel. To afford a family, and live the way I want, I will have to give up my dreams over the next five years."

Instead of thinking seesaw, think how you can have both: Both sides of the seesaw rise. Once you reframe the conversation you have with choices, you will start to see a way to have both.

Once Oliver reframed this, he saw he could have both. Four years later, he is married and has met every one of his financial guideposts over the last five years. What he did was fundamentally course correct so that marriage and having a personal life could fit into his financial plan. It's a real source of joy in his life, and that matters.

That's what we mean when we say that financial planning is not all black and white and numbers—it's making sure that a plan is flexible enough to allow you to make changes so that you're living the life you want along the way.

Your "Real Wealth" (Money Is Only One Asset)

Most people treat "wealth" as if it were a single number. But real wealth is a portfolio: energy, skills, relationships, experiences, reputation, and, yes, money. Those assets interact. When one improves, the others usually get easier.

Money is fuel, not a trophy. You use it to create freedom, which means more choices.

So some spending is not "bad." It's an investment. Paying for the gym, better food, therapy, a course, a certification, a hobby that keeps you sane, or a flight to see people you love can be a wealth move when it matches your values and strengthens your future choices.

Here's the upgrade: You can invest in your life and make the money side smarter at the same time.

— Application Box —
Amin's "Real Wealth" Exercise

Before you spend, ask:

- Does this purchase increase my options for freedom later? Options can look like higher earnings, better health, stronger relationships, less stress, more confidence, or fewer future problems.
- Can I fund it without interest or chaos? If the purchase creates debt stress, it is not an investment. It is a trade.

A Simple Example: Movement

Low physical activity increases long-term health risks and medical costs. Regular movement reduces those risks and supports both physical and mental well-being.

Translation: The gym is not "just a gym." It's a plan to prevent future medical bills.

The "Return Stack" (How To Make The Same Life Purchase Pay Twice)

Once something passes the "real wealth" test, stack the return.

Return 1: Life return

This is the direct improvement to your life, health, skill, confidence, time, relationships, or reduced stress.
If the purchase makes your daily life better or your future self stronger, it passes this layer.

Return 2: Money return

This is the financial impact over time.
Does this reduce future costs (like medical bills, mistakes, or inefficiencies)?

Does it increase future income (better skills, better opportunities)?
If it saves you money later or helps you earn more, it passes this layer.

Return 3: Payment return

This is how you execute the purchase.
Even if you're going to spend the money anyway, how you pay still matters.
Can you get cash back, rewards, discounts, or perks?
Can you avoid interest completely?
This is about capturing value at the moment of payment instead of leaving it on the table.

If you're going to spend the money anyway, route it through your best deal: the strongest discount, perks, and cash back you can get.

Practical Moves That Make "Investing In Yourself" Cheaper

Use this checklist the same way a chief financial officer (CFO) would:

- Price check in three minutes
  - Always check for student discounts, employer benefits, community programs, ClassPass-style alternatives, and off-peak memberships.
  - Do the annual plan versus monthly plan math.
- Ask for a free version first
  - Libraries are not just books anymore. In 2025, libraries hit 820.5 million digital checkouts through Libby and Sora, and usage keeps rising.[12] That means your

"I should read more" goal might be a free habit, not a $28-per-hardcover habit.

- Use the best payment tool
  - Use your best cash back card for the category.

A Quick Story (With A Small Truth Bomb)

Two people buy the same gym membership.

Person A buys it, feels guilty, pays with whatever card, forgets about it, and carries a balance.

Person B treats it like an asset: sets a schedule, tracks usage, pays with a card that rewards it, and never pays a dollar of interest.

Totally different outcomes.

The difference is not discipline. It is designed.

Try This Week: One Real Wealth Upgrade

Pick one purchase you already believe improves your life (health, skill, relationships).

- Name the why (one sentence).
  - "I'm investing in fitness to buy energy and prevent future problems."
- Do a five-minute price check (without overthinking).
  - Check library/free resources first (books, audiobooks, classes).
  - Ask for student/employer/community discounts (most exist; few are advertised).
  - Compare monthly versus annual pricing and choose the better value.
- Pay it the smart way.
  - Route it through your best rewards and protect the win by avoiding interest (set autopay to the statement

balance). If you can't pay it off this month, redesign the purchase until it fits your cash flow.

- Measure the real return.
    - Write one line: Did this increase my options?
    - If yes, keep it in your wealth portfolio. If no, downgrade or cut it.

That's how spending stops being emotional and becomes a portfolio decision: You live now, and you build, on purpose.

You Don't Have To Give Up Living To Have A Life

It's easy to transform a person's life if they're willing to scrape by, eating instant ramen.

But it is a lot more complicated for most people. They have their wants and needs, and they have things in their lives that go wrong: They have a problem with a child, parent, or loved one; an illness comes up; they lose their job; or a marriage or relationship ends.

These rough patches are all part of the normal course of life. But with a solid plan, you can deal with the chasms, bumps, and potholes that come up along the way. Making that happen is what's important in our work with people. It's how we continually transform lives.

One of our long-term clients is also a good friend—Aidan, who met Al when he was a young physician. At that time, medicine was going through a lot of changes, and many popular influencers were telling young doctors to pay off their debts and hunker down because things were not going to be the same and physicians would be hitting hard times. They were really spreading panic.

Aidan was just starting out in his specialty practice when he came in to meet with Al. We really connected, although our advice to him was the total opposite of anything he had heard from others. We told him to keep his debt and to look to his cash flow. He asked us, "Why is everyone out there telling me something different?"

We explained that influencers give advice that sounds easy, simple, and feel-good to people. Influencers patronize people and don't tell them what real finance is. Al said, "You do it our way, and chances are, that you'll get wherever you want in life." Over the next twenty years, Aidan not only created a successful practice but also founded other businesses. He is very well-off today, but he's still that down-to-earth guy. More importantly, he lives life the way he wants.

When Al married some years ago, he asked Aidan and his wife to his wedding. The chief operating officer (COO) of Al's former company happened to be sitting with them at the reception. Aidan turned to the COO and said, "You know, Al Zdenek is the best thing that ever happened to me." The COO was kind of stunned, especially since Aidan's wife was right next to him and was listening to the conversation.

Half-jokingly, he said, "I'm sure you meant except for your wife Kayleigh, right?"

Without even a beat, Aidan said, "No, I mean her too." She didn't argue.

— Application Box —

The Conversation To Have With Yourself: Write The Script Beforehand

Motivation is unreliable. Planning the conversation with yourself is powerful.

Behavioral research shows that simple "if, then" plans (implementation intentions) reliably increase follow-through: If x happens, then I will do *y*.[13]

This isn't "being perfect." It's removing decision-making from the moments you're most likely to slip, when you're tired, hungry, bored, stressed, or one click away from "confirm purchase."

Amin's Actions You Can Take (Real Life Version)

Spending And Shopping

- If I want to buy something online, then I wait twenty-four hours and recheck tomorrow.
- If I put something into my cart, then I must remove one item before checkout.
- If I'm buying something over $50, then I check: *used, refurbished, library, borrow, rent first.*
- If I'm bored scrolling, then I exit the app and do a two-minute "money glance" first.

Food And Convenience

- If I open a delivery app, then I choose pickup, or I cook what I already have.
- If I'm craving coffee out, then I make coffee at home and keep the "coffee money" for a Friday treat.

Friends And Social Plans

- If friends suggest an expensive plan, then I offer a cheaper option first.
- If the plan involves a cover/fees, then I say "yes" only if it fits my "fun ceiling" (the amount I put aside for fun) for the week.

Paydays And Autopilot

- If money hits my account, then bills due before next payday get scheduled immediately.
- If I get unexpected money (refund/gift), then 50 percent goes to savings before I touch the rest.

Subscriptions And Microleaks

- If I start a free trial, then I cancel it the same day and keep access until it ends.
- If I haven't used a subscription in thirty days, then I downgrade or pause it for one month.
- If a subscription price increases, then I review it that week—no "silent yes."

Buy Now, Pay Later And Debt Drift

- If the checkout offers installments, then I treat it like full price and only proceed if I could pay it today.
- If I already have one installment running, then I don't start another until it's done.

Strong, Clean Phrases You Can Actually Say

- "I'm down. I'm just keeping it lean this week."
- "I'm skipping this round—save me for the next one."
- "I'm doing a twenty-four-hour rule. If I still want it tomorrow, I'll buy it."

- "I'm keeping my spending tight today—what's the best low-key option?"
- "I'm choosing quality over impulse. Let's pick a better move."
- "I'm on a 'no autopilot' week. I'm saying 'yes' to fewer things."

CakeClub Slices

- Practical and emotional obstacles prevent you from making better financial choices, living the lifestyle you want now, and achieving financial freedom.
- "Real wealth" is more than just how much money you have.
- Try the "real wealth" exercise.
- Determine a "real wealth" upgrade once in a while.
- Determine the conversations you have with yourself.

…say, "What do you want?" hear the goals … on those areas, and take your money to invest. Rather, w… aspect of your financial life. We are out to find more free cash flow… cash flow is cash left after all bills have been paid. To find the most free cash flow you can, you must look at every part of your financial life.

If we find more free cash flow working with you (and there has never been a case in which we have not), you can spend this excess cash flow on your lifestyle. Or, if you save and invest it, you could:

- Achieve your short- and long-term financial goals more quickly
- Have more wealth at the end of the time frame of your plan
- Reduce the risk in your investment portfolio

…ur philosophy is that we don't believe that penny-pinching—as we have said before, skipping Starbucks to make coffee at home or giving up whatever it is that makes you happy—is the way to live your life and take on the challenge of creating and achieving a financial plan.

Our philosophy is that if you make better financial decisions around your cash flow, then you'll waste less money on avoidable expenses and will give less money to the government. That will empower you to have that money for your lifestyle now, to save and build your wealth for how you want to live in retirement, and to achieve financial independence.

We call this approach to generating more cash flow the Integrated Cash Flow Management Approach. Our personal financial planning methodology is the Wealth Building Formula. This chapter will be

3

Becoming The Master Of Your Cash Flow

Number one, cash is king.

—Jack Welch, former GE CEO

At CakeClub, o

focused on these two approaches, which are designed to make you become a master of your cash flow, achieve the way you wish to live now and achieve short- or long-term goals like financial freedom.

The Two Kinds Of Personal Financial Planners

There are two types of personal financial planners. One is called a goals-based planner. If you go to a goals-based planner, you will be asked what kind of goals you have in life. You might say, "I want to be retired by forty-five," "I want a vacation home in Colorado," "I want my children to be educated," or "I want a larger home." The goals-based planner will help you calculate the numbers for the different "pots of money" you need for those goals. Then the conversation becomes about how much you have to save for them and how to let them invest your money.

We are cash-flow planners, which is the second type. Cash-flow planners are much less common than goals-based planners. A cash-flow planner will ask the same questions as a goals-based planner because it is important to know your goals. But there's one big difference: We just don't [illegible] you give us, concentrate [illegible] look at every [illegible] Free

We will discuss all of the above and what they mean as we progress through this book. But let's concentrate now on finding more free cash flow to invest, or what we call "investable cash."

For example, if you came to us with the goals we listed above but neglected to mention debt, insurance, where you work, or how you work, we would explore those areas with you. If you have a business, we'd want to know how the business is running, how you are pricing your product or service, and what profit you are earning. If you have a job, we'd ask how you're negotiating your contract or compensation. How are you choosing your benefits and determining the contributions and investment selections of your 401(k)? We look at all these aspects of your financial life because doing so helps us find more investable cash.

Financial choices don't have just one effect on your finances; any one decision can affect many areas of your financial life. These decisions can use more of your cash flow or provide more investable cash. It is your choice.

For example, if you're buying an apartment or house, probably the first thing you'll ask yourself is, "Can I afford the mortgage?" But buying a house is just not a cash flow decision or a debt decision. It's also an investment decision, an insurance decision, an estate decision, and a tax decision. There are many financial areas that your purchase of a house is going to affect, and if you're not looking at all of those areas, you may not make the best financial choice—the choice that will help you to keep building wealth, to get to your goals in life, and to live the life you wish now.

We've touched on this analogy before, but properly executed, the Integrated Cash Flow Management Approach comes down to running your finances like a well-run company does. When you think of a well-run company like Apple, they have the same issues that we all have. When they make a financial decision, it affects many, many areas.

When Al worked at Merck & Co. Inc. in their corporate tax department, they wanted to build a plant in another state, which is somewhat like buying a house. But that is where the similarity ends. As a well-run company, they considered all of the areas of financial impact, unlike most home buyers.

As we said before, it's not only a decision as to whether you can afford the house itself (cash flow) but also the other issues it affects: It's an investment decision, an insurance decision, a tax decision, a debt decision, and an estate decision. Companies don't call it an "estate" decision; to them, it's a "shareholder wealth" decision. They take this all into account to make the best financial choice.

The Integrated Cash Flow Management Approach is making decisions with the same mindset that well-run businesses apply to their financial situations, using the best practices toward managing their cash flow, finding more investable cash, and growing more wealth.

We Work With Smart People . . . And Make Them Smarter

We meet many individuals of all ages—executives, entrepreneurs, business owners, physicians, and professionals—and these people are very bright. Most are in their late twenties to late thirties; have become skilled at managing their businesses, careers, and professions; and are often among the very best at what they do. But what they normally have not mastered is their cash flow.

As we have said before, time and time again, clients who are very successful in life come to meet with us and say, "I visit my accountant at the end of the year to do my tax return. They tell me how much I've earned and how much I owe, and I think to myself, *I made all that money? What did I do with it?*"

Most don't know how to control and become masters of their cash flow. But through our Integrated Cash Flow Management Approach, we make them the masters of their money. We give them control over their cash flow so that they can preserve their wealth or build additional wealth to do the things in life they want, now or in the future.

A good example is Luna, a young nurse who was stressed and anxious, having accumulated $50,000 in student debt. Like many, she felt that she had to pay this off as soon as possible, and that it would be the most responsible and safest decision. But her problem was that she was left with no cash at the end of the month, no way to build an emergency fund for surprise expenses, and certainly no way to save in the hospital savings plan. She didn't know how to get off this monthly treadmill.

We showed her some alternatives of paying off the debt over a longer period of time and renegotiating the rates on the loans. Immediately, she was able to save $500 per month. After building a small emergency fund, she started to contribute to the savings plan at work. Saving there gave her tax benefits (generally, contributions to savings plans are tax-deductible). She put away her tax savings too.

From not being able to save anything, she was saving almost $10,000 per year and still paying off her loans. She was safer in that she had emergency cash, but was also saving toward her financial goals using the power of compounding to grow her savings and also using the "Tax Savings Savings Effect," both to be discussed in more depth in later chapters.

Making better financial choices and also understanding what it means for your big picture is extremely important. That's what the Integrated Cash Flow Management Approach is all about: making you a master of your money.

We're not out to make you CPAs, attorneys, insurance agents, or other experts like that. We're out to make sure that you know how to find and use reputable experts, where your money is going, and where you are right now, that you have the wealth you need at any time in the future, and that you know how to manage and build that wealth.

Knowledge is power—and who better to have power over your future than you?

Debt Isn't Always The Enemy

Keep in mind that there's nothing wrong with paying off debt. It's wrong, though, to pay it off without considering how that affects your current wealth and cash flow generation now and in the future.

We think people would probably agree that Warren Buffett is a pretty savvy business investor—and Warren Buffett's companies have debt. Well-run companies have debt. They have debt for a reason; by balancing debt with what is held in assets, more wealth can be generated.

We're not encouraging you to go out and incur debt just to have it, much less to run up credit card debt for frivolous consumption. But exploring the opportunities of having debt may allow you to balance more wealth generation, and is a savvy thing to consider. We'll talk more extensively about using debt smarter in a later chapter.

We do see a couple of different kinds of clients whose cash flow management problems get them into difficulties.

The first group is those who've just come out of high school or college—professionals or young executives, for instance, and who suddenly start making real money. They get their first paycheck, they're feeling good, and they are inclined to treat themselves to some rewards: a new car, new wardrobe, high-end restaurant meals, and travel.

They run up some big bills, and then all of a sudden, they find out that cash is tight. Normally, when you sit down with those people and make them aware of how it has happened, it's pretty easy to correct.

But other, more ingrained habits—like spending more than you should over a career's worth of time—aren't so easy to break. We gradually get acclimated to this way of living; we get used to keeping up with our friends, or there are things that we want and think we should have.

We're hoping that the next bonus or raise from our job or our business is going to make everything OK, but it never quite catches up.

Another type of person is what we'll call a "person of circumstances"—and those circumstances are sometimes not good. They've lived for years with excess cash flow. They've lived within a certain budget. They've even saved some money on the side.

But then something happens: They lose their jobs, or their business falters. They have a tough time finding a job. Eventually they do find one, but they've had this interruption in cash flow, and if they didn't have adequate savings put aside, that interruption can really damage what they have built up. They still have the groceries to pay for, the house to support, the kids to educate, and the mortgage to pay.

The tragedy is when you have a person who has been a manager or business owner who has lived a nice lifestyle but hasn't saved enough because they didn't know how much they needed to save or assume that their business or company pension would cover their retirement. Suddenly, in their mid- to late fifties, they're thrown out of work or suffer a bad patch, and all of a sudden, their retirement plans evaporate.

This is not uncommon. In fact, we've seen this every time there's been a crash in the market, whether it's been the 2008 crash or the most recent crash of 2020. In each of these, we've met with people who had been on track for their financial plan and time frame, and all of a sudden their 401(k)s became "201(k)s"—they got cut in half. They found out that they had to work longer, take a second job, or else have less cash flow in their retirement years.

Lucas was a client we had in 2017 who was in the real estate business. He was a mid-level executive in a big firm that built shopping malls and bought and sold very large properties. He and his wife, Olivia, enjoyed a nice lifestyle. They'd invested in some of these shopping center and industrial park partnerships because the company always kept shares for executive retirement. What they didn't realize is that they had all their eggs in one basket.

All of a sudden, the 2020 crash and recession hit, and what suffered the most at that time was real estate. A lot of people ended up giving their real estate back to the banks and declaring bankruptcy. Lucas was forty-one; Olivia was a little younger. All of the properties that had made them look good on paper were suddenly worth a whole lot less. What was worse was that his company had to downsize, so they asked him to leave. Now he had no income and an almost-worthless portfolio.

Working The Numbers

We had Lucas and Olivia calculate the amount of wealth they actually needed to live the lifestyle they wished. Focusing on their current holdings for the first time, we began to go through their portfolio and to decide what they could sell, as well as what they couldn't or shouldn't. Some properties they had to sell at a sacrifice, but it was essential to diversify so that they could have cash flow to get back to the life they wanted to live now and also be able to retire down the line.

At that time, Lucas didn't think he was going to be able to retire until his mid-seventies. But through our Integrated Cash Flow Management Approach and by creating their Wealth Building Formula (which we'll get into in a later chapter), within three or four years, we were able to make up a good deal of the assets they'd had before, and we restored their cash flow. He and his wife have now been enjoying the life they wanted.

Again, here were intelligent people who'd made some poor financial choices that came close to ruining them, largely because they were poorly educated about finances and managing cash flow. Poor financial choices can come back to haunt you, even if you're doing well.

It's All About Your Choices

After some years out of college, you might finally be offered job opportunities you like with different compensation levels. You have choices to make; one employer might offer $100,000 a year, another might offer $90,000, and a third might offer to pay you $105,000 a year. If you don't understand finance and can't adequately judge the benefits and other opportunities that each of these employers is offering, in addition to salary, you can make the wrong financial decision.

The employer that offers $105,000 may not have a pension plan or other benefits like helping to pay off student loans, for instance. That means you have to fund those items for yourself, which might effectively cut the cash flow you're making down to $85,000, whereas the company that offered you what looked like less might actually be offering you more once you factor in those extras.

It's the same way with a business. When people start businesses, they normally go through what we call the "break-even process." They say to themselves, "I have overhead like rent, salaries to pay people, utilities, and other costs," and they can list these exactly. Their thinking is, "If I bring in enough sales to cover expenses, I've broken even," and they think they're succeeding.

This is not realistic. Success doesn't mean that you just pay for your overhead; it means that you're also making the money that's going to allow you to live the lifestyle you wish, pay your taxes, and be able to save for retirement or be financially independent in the time frame you choose. That's why, when you're making your budget for a business, you should add what you have to earn as a salary, what you have to pay in taxes, and what you need to put aside annually for your financial independence.

Most business owners don't do that, so they have a business that goes on for years and years and may grow very large, but they haven't amassed the savings that they should have to ensure that they're going to accomplish what they want. Granted, their business may be worth something someday. But it's a big danger to bet your future on what your business might be worth someday. You could hit a rough patch in the economy or face stiff competition. You or other key people could fall ill, which could hurt the value of the business and ruin your plans for an early exit, especially when you're close to financial freedom.

The bottom line is that the vast majority of people don't have enough financial education or financial background to make informed choices about their finances, nor do they take sufficient time to sit down and really look at, "What kind of cash flow will I have coming in? And what do I have to do with it?"

The Funnels

The analogy we use to describe how most people think about their cash flow is the "three funnel system," or simply "the funnels." Most people think of the cash flowing into their lives like it's coming to them through a funnel: their paycheck. Withholding taxes for the government come out of that check in the first funnel, as well as unemployment taxes and all the other taxes the government imposes, so already you see a lot less money in your hands than your salary once it's gone through this funnel.

What's left then flows into the second funnel, which is the "things we have to pay" funnel. That would include your mortgage, student loans, car loans, and credit cards. This funnel is your debt.

The money that flows from the debt funnel flows into the last funnel, which is what we'd call "lifestyle"—it covers all other expenses like food, utilities, vacations—expenses that are part of life. Whatever is left after this last funnel—if there's anything—is what people see as money they can then save for their future.

Figure 1: The Cash Flow Funnels
How People Normally Think Of Cash Flow And Saving Income

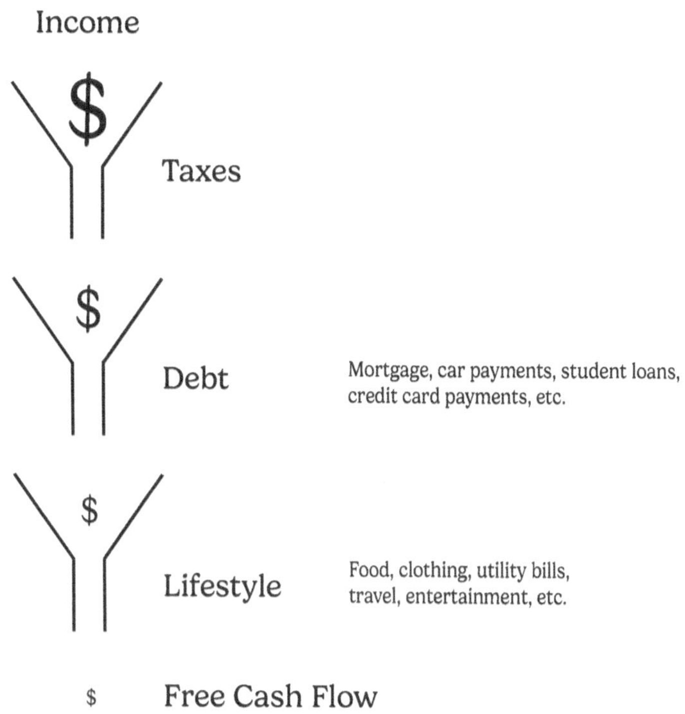

But a well-run business sees cash flow very differently. A well-run business has the same three funnels. Money flows into the first funnel in the form of sales, and like everyone, businesses have to pay taxes out of that.

The second funnel is where they pay debt.

The last funnel, the one individuals think of as "lifestyle" is what a company calls "operations." They have to pay for the heat, lights, employee salaries, benefits, and other costs.

What is left is profit, or earnings per share.

Stockholders like to see share values rise, and if earnings per share go up year after year, that means the stock price also tends to go up.

If earnings per share are flat, that could mean the stock price is flat. If earnings per share go down, then your stock price most likely will go down.

What happens to the executive team at those companies whose stock goes down every year? They get fired. So they have a vested interest in making sure that after the money goes through those three funnels, the money at the end is a higher amount than it was last year, so that the earnings per share are higher than they were the previous year.

How do executives do that? When the money first starts coming into the first funnel, they're already starting to make choices like, "Do I open up that factory, hire this person, fire that person?" They want to make sure the bottom line will be higher than it was last year. They are focused on a goal, and their choices are aligned with that goal.

Most people don't run their cash flow like well-run businesses. Money comes in, it goes out, and they hope that there's something left at the end of the year. Companies don't think like that. They target the bottom line or profit.

What you want to do is to target your money as a well-run business does. You want to say, "If I have a certain amount of cash flow now, and I want it to be more, this much has to be left over after my expenses. If it isn't, then either my expenses have to change, or the way I make money has to change." That's the way to run your cash flow like a well-run business.

To increase personal cash flow, you might ask for a raise, take up a side gig like driving for Uber or DoorDash, become a part-time real estate agent, or start a side venture like helping businesses build websites, or become a part-time administrative assistant. Target the cash flow and go after it.

If you find that you're frustrated, you're stressed and anxious about your cash flow, and there doesn't seem to be much (if any) extra at the end of the year, then even if you have a good amount of savings, you could see your savings amount stagnate or go down, leaving you without the cash flow you need.

But you have a choice. You can go year after year, hoping that your goal will be achieved by the end of the year, or you can start to target the amounts that you need and make sure that you take action and make choices aligned with a sound financial plan to hit the target.

Know What You Are Spending: Create A Spending Plan, Not A Budget

If you don't know how much you're spending, how can you plan your wealth and your future cash flow for you and your loved ones? It's like deciding to just get in your car and drive without knowing how much fuel you have. This does not mean you necessarily have to spend less; just know what you are spending.

How do you accomplish this? The first thought you might have is "I need a budget," and sigh deeply. Most people hate budgeting because it feels restrictive, time-consuming, and judgmental. Money and budgeting cause more arguments between spouses and partners than almost anything else.

In this book, we stopped calling it a "budget" and renamed it a "spending plan." A spending plan lets you choose what matters to you. You control it. It creates clarity by showing what comes in and what goes out each month. The amount of detail you wish is up to you.

Working over the years with many users, we developed three types of spending plans. The first we call the "quick" plan. Look at your bank statement(s) at the end of the month. What came in, what went out, and what was left? Hopefully, there was something left over, and if not, you could then review the statement, see why, and adjust if you wanted.

The second one is the "bucket" spending plan. Use simple buckets instead of detailed line items, such as:

- fixed (same each month: rent, mortgage, loan payments)
- flexible (where you have the choice)
- fun (guilt-free spending you enjoy)
- future (target amounts for saving/investing)

You get to name the buckets and what goes in each. You can name the buckets as actual expense categories, but if you do, choose no more than six to ten. It might get too burdensome after that. This isn't about restriction. It's about control. Once you label it, you can choose what you spend here or not.

The third option is the "really, do I need this?" plan or the "detailed" spending plan, a more expansive report with twenty-plus expense categories. Accountants and engineers really love this. Their spouses usually don't.

As you might expect, most users go with the first two. The third is chosen by very few. Amin uses the "bucket" option.

Time is often the biggest objection we hear. But this can be solved via automation. Most software (and phone apps like the personal finance CakeClub app) can be connected to your bank accounts, so transactions are sent directly to the software and automatically categorized in a spending plan.

The last part of having an effective spending plan is reviewing it periodically. We suggest reviewing it once a month. Once in place, it should take little time to review. If you are reviewing it with a partner or spouse, be patient and kind. No arguing.

A spending plan may not be fun, but it beats feeling restricted, judged, or out of control.

You don't necessarily hate managing money. You hate being told what you cannot do. A spending plan works because it puts you back in control and aligns money with the life you want.

Before we create a spending plan with people, we ask what they spend per month, even if they have to guess. Most have no idea what their spending is. We work with them to put together the numbers on what they spent for that month or over a three-month or a six-month period. They need to get out those bank statements and follow the cash flow.

As CPAs, we can also calculate approximate overall spending for you, but it is important that you know where your spending is. Is what you have coming in adequate to cover your expenses, or are you borrowing to make ends meet? That's the first step; knowledge is power.

Then we go into our spending plan process. Once they have one of the spending plan options in place, we can see how much they earned for the year and how much they paid in taxes. If they had to borrow money at the end of the year or during the year, and they had to take it from their savings, we know that they're not actually meeting their cash flow needs. If we see that they have a surplus, then we can see if it's enough for them to live the lifestyle they wish, now and in the future. This also allows us to check for wasteful spending and opportunities for finding investable cash.

In any case, just as in a well-run company, it's critical to really know your numbers. It is also very important to check this annually: Revisit how much money you actually need for the lifestyle you're living, and see what's left. Companies that do not know how much they are spending are in big trouble.

People often underestimate; we had a couple who estimated their household spending at $150,000 per year. But when we looked at what they earned and what they paid in taxes, we found that they could not account for some $50,000. Once that cash flow spending is visible, we can see more clearly what is needed, where the problems are, and, even more importantly, where the opportunities lie.

People lead busy lives and don't pay attention to where their money is going. Sometimes it's going places they aren't even aware of. When it's pointed out to them, they often realize, "I don't really need that," or "I'm overpaying for this," and we can find them more cash flow.

One example is home insurance, especially for someone who owns more than one or two homes. We've had clients who, unbeknownst to them, were paying $10,000 for their home insurance. They didn't realize that when they'd made a claim two or three years ago, the insurance company didn't like it and had jacked up their rates. Too often, these kinds of bills are put on autopay and never reviewed. With those clients, we were able to reduce their home insurance bills from $10,000 to $2,000 a year, with better protection. This is not unusual.

Are You Maximizing Your Benefits?

Another example of a common problem is a manager who, because she didn't understand the benefits her company was offering, like pension or savings plan choices, wasn't actually fully participating in them, even though she thought that she was.

Mia came to see us when she was in her late thirties and had been working with her company for a while. We pointed out to her that there was a particular deferred compensation plan that would allow her to put away her total bonuses for the year. This strategy would save her over $5,000 a year in taxes. She didn't need all the pay she made, and this way, she could add another $10,000 or more per year to her savings without even feeling it—a nice investable cash find.

Another recent example was a couple who overpaid their taxes by almost $6,000. The CPA preparing their tax returns did not realize the error. It was not until we reviewed their income taxes that we told them to have their CPA contact the government and get the cash back.

People get busy and don't focus on where they're spending money or who's sending them the bills except when it's outlandish or their cash is tight. That's why we're always able to find money for people for investable cash that they don't even know they have.

In fact, in thirty years in business, having spoken to literally hundreds of people, we have never—not once—been unable to find, at minimum, a couple of thousand of dollars a year, and sometimes much more, in excess cash flow. In some cases, millions of dollars are found through better tax planning, reviewing benefits, looking at how a business owner is running his or her company, or scrutinizing expenses.

— Application Box —
Temptation Bundling (Make The "Should" Feel Like A "Want")

Sometimes the issue isn't knowledge. It's energy.

Researchers tested a simple strategy: Pair something you *want* with something you *should* do. It's called temptation bundling, and studies show it can increase follow-through on behaviors like exercise.[14]

Money version:

- Only listen to your favorite podcast while doing your ten-minute spending plan check.
- Only buy your "fun coffee" on the day you make your automatic savings transfer.
- Only scroll guilt-free after you've paid bills and moved your savings money to your savings account.

This isn't bribing yourself.

It's designing a system your brain will actually stick with.

If you feel "randomly" tempted to spend, it is rarely random. Your feed is a shopping mall with better lighting.

Try it this week for fifteen minutes:

- Unfollow or mute three accounts that trigger spending.
- Turn off shopping push notifications.

- Delete saved credit card information from one store, just one.
- Add one "replace, repair, borrow, rent" option before you buy.

You are not depriving yourself. You are removing noise, so your best choice becomes easier by default, which is the point.

CakeClub Slices

- There are two kinds of financial planners/advisers: goals oriented and cash-flow oriented. Choose the cash-flow-oriented person.
- Debt isn't always the enemy (will discuss further in chapter 8) and can be powerful in growing wealth.
- The "funnels" are how people normally think of cash flow and savings income. Learn to control your funnel.
- Create a spending plan, not a budget. Choose and be in control of how you spend.
- Complete the temptation bundling exercise but do not deprive yourself.

4

The Wealth Building Formula

Your economic security does not lie in your job; it lies in your own power to produce—to think, to learn, to create, to adapt. That's true financial independence.

—STEPHEN R. COVEY, PRODUCTIVITY AUTHOR

Do you remember the *Downton Abbey* movies and television series? A favorite quote from a favorite character, the Dowager Countess, played by the late Dame Maggie Smith, was the ironic: "Oh, good, let's talk about money."[15]

The countess was above such money talk, but we are not.

Money is not a vulgar subject. On the contrary, it is an essential topic if you want to have cash flow and time to enjoy the lifestyle you desire.

Our philosophy is that people should live the lifestyle they wish for now; if they focus on their cash flow and don't waste money on imprudent expenses or pay excess taxes and make better financial choices, this should be possible.

We've explained our Integrated Cash Flow Management Approach and how to view your financial choices through the lens of a well-run business. The next financial detail to ascertain is how much wealth you need now or "core" wealth—wealth that will keep you financially independent. Our methodology for doing this: the Wealth Building Formula.

You'll recall the three funnels we talked about in the previous chapter and that well-run businesses look at cash flow by targeting their spending because they have to make sure the bottom line is going to be higher than it was last year.

Individuals, on the other hand, may just hope the extra money's there; too often, they're not aware whether it is or isn't.

The Wealth Building Formula provides an individual with benchmarks on what wealth is needed and the way to make the best financial decisions consistently to grow and retain that wealth. Let's deal with benchmarks first. Benchmarks are what well-run companies have that individuals don't; Apple and other successful companies all have financial benchmarks or key performance indicators (KPIs) that allow them to assess things like, "Are we doing better than our peers or worse than our peers? Are we hitting our targets?" Among their benchmarks might be earnings per share, return on equity, or other measures.

As individuals, we don't think in terms of earnings per share. Most people don't even know how much they need to save. They don't have a long-term investment return objective or rate of return needed from their investment portfolios to make it all work. They just hope it's there. For example, with investments, they just look to see, "Did I do better than the S&P 500 this quarter?" That's not the same thing as creating your target. But you can't reach a target without a plan that provides you with benchmarks and a way to make the right financial decisions.

The Wealth Building Formula allows people to put their goals into exact numbers. It creates a clear process for making good financial decisions—one that lets them see where they are on their roadmap.

When do they want to be financially independent? What about in five years, ten years? Are they on the right track?

The Wealth Building Formula looks at what cash flow you need today to live the life you wish. As an example, let's assume you needed $125,000 a year to live—to pay your taxes, to cover expenses, to meet short-term goals, and to save toward building your wealth. You're bringing in this income either through working for someone or via your business. But someday, you want to have the option to leave your job or sell that business, either to do something else or to retire. If you can get that same $125,000 you require every year from your investments, adjusted for inflation (you can count on inflation rising each year), then you've achieved financial freedom. You can do whatever you want. You don't have to go to work. You can take more risks, open a business, and have the option not to deal with anyone you don't want to.

The Wealth Building Formula is a straightforward equation:

C x T x %Return = $$$

where *C* is investable cash you must save annually to achieve the amount of wealth you need to generate cash flow and *T* is the time frame in which you want to gain your financial independence. *%Return* is the long-term investment return objective that you need (from your investment portfolio) to make sure this all works and that the cash flow you are generating equals the cash flow that you'll need in today's dollars at the point when you retire or decide to do something else. Finally, *$$$* is wealth that will generate the annual cash flow needed for financial independence.

When we work with clients, we use this equation to make sure that each of them has their own personalized Wealth Building Formula and their own benchmarks to track.

What kind of cash flow do you need to make sure that you can live the lifestyle you wish? What does that equate to in wealth? What types of investments do you need so your amount of wealth generates the needed cash flow? What kind of time frame are we talking about to get to that point?

Then, what percentage return do you need? What long-term investment return objective should you have so that you can properly construct your portfolio and balance it with the risk you wish to take (which we will talk about in another chapter)?

Everyone Is Different

Knowing your personal Wealth Building Formula is critical to achieving the financial independence you want, within a time frame that's workable for your goals and how you wish to live now.

Once you've nailed that down, then the second and just as important part is *working* your formula. How do you work it? When you're making financial decisions, you measure them against the yardstick of your Wealth Building Formula.

The numbers represented in the equation *C x T x %Return = $$$* are variables. A change in one of the variables on the left side of the equation will have an effect on the right side—the cash flow for which you are planning. A change on the right side of the equation—the wealth to generate the cash flow needed—will have an effect on one or all of the variables on the left side. Knowing what these variables are, the effects caused by changes in any one of them, and targeting and keeping track of them just as a well-run business does will allow you to make the right financial choices.

Let's look at an example: If you can save more than you target annually to *C* (your investable cash), then the *T* (time) to get there will be reduced, you can earn less percent return, or the *$$$* (wealth) you are targeting could be more.

Wealth Building Formula

C x T x %Return = $$$

Investable cash x time x percent return = annual cash flow for financial independence

How Does It Work?

If you have to save *$10,000* per year (*C*) but you actually save *$12,500* (more than you have to), the following can happen:

↑C x ↓T x ↓%Return = ↑$$$

T can *decrease, %Return* can *decrease*, or you have *more* cash flow ($$$) due to *increased* wealth. By adding more than what was required to your wealth, you could decrease your time to independence (*T*) or you could reduce your percent return needed from your investments to keep the same cash flow (*$$$*).

Conversely, say that you have to save $10,000 per year (*C*), but actually you save only $7,500 (less than you have to), the following can happen:

↓C x ↑T x ↑%Return = ↓$$$

T can *increase, percent return* can *increase*, or you have *less* cash flow due to *decreased* wealth.

If you save less than your annual target to *C* or use money from your wealth for some purpose, then *T* will be increased (delaying your independence), you will have to raise the *percent return* (thus increasing risk) to achieve your *cash flow*, or your cash flow (*$$$*) will be less.

↓C x ↑T x ↑%Return = ↓$$$

Any financial choice increases or decreases *C*. Knowing this will allow you to make choices knowing that you are increasing or decreasing *T* or percent return in your portfolio. Or, if you choose to keep *T* and percent return the same, you will affect *$$$*—your targeted wealth.

Got it?

Here's another view of how the formula works: A financial choice comes along—you want to put a $50,000 addition or improvement in your apartment or home. You could go out and borrow the money, or you could take the money from the *C* or investable wealth you have.

If you borrow the money, you're going to pay it back over a period of time. You will not have to decrease *C* (or wealth), so you do not have to increase *T* (time) or percent return. Borrowing the money does not decrease *C*, and thus your formula is unaffected. But if you take the improvement funds from your *C*, then you will have to increase *T* or percent return for it not to affect your *$$$* (wealth). We are assuming in this example that you will be able to absorb the annual payments of debt from your current cash flow without affecting your savings target each year.

By the way, this is what we mean by "working" your Wealth Building Formula to make the best financial decisions for yourself.

As another example, say that you have a $500,000 mortgage on your residence that costs you about $25,000 a year. You're one of those people who decides, "You know what? I'm going to pay it off quicker. I have a good job. I have the extra cash flow for it. So I'm not only going to pay my $25,000, I'm going to pay an extra $10,000 each year." Deciding to accelerate their mortgage payments is a very common choice people make.

But suppose that instead of putting that $10,000 into the house, you added it to your *C*. This might get you to your financial goals quicker, or you might have more wealth to generate cash flow ($$$) when you get to the end of your *T* and reach retirement or independence. People accelerate payments all of the time and don't realize that they are just adding more time in which they "have" to work, are increasing the risk in their portfolios, or are setting themselves up to have less cash flow when they want to retire or want to do something else.

Knowledge Is Power—And It Gives You Options

We had a client who was just getting out of his residency program and had significant debt. He wanted to pay off his student loans over five years. By working his Wealth Building Formula, we were able to show him that if he did that, he wasn't going to be able to save sufficient money out of his cash flow to support his long-term financial plan.

However, he had the option to pay off the loans over twenty-five years, which meant the yearly payments were a lot less, and thus he'd have more money to save now. If he chose that option and added it to his *C*, his time frame became shorter because his cash flow became a lot higher, and he didn't have to get as high a percent return on his portfolio, which meant he could invest his money at less risk.

This same physician also had two car loans that he was trying to pay off as quickly as possible. We showed him that he could save $10,000 of additional investable cash per year by paying these car loans off slower so that his payments weren't as high, and he could add the excess cash flow to his *C*, which got him to his goals faster.

He's been a client for twenty-five years and is now enjoying financial independence. We recently got an email from him, thanking us for transforming his attitude toward money and his life all those years ago.

There's a lot of conflicting advice on personal finance, but it's important to remember that most of these pundits and "experts" are speaking generally to the masses. The fact is, the same financial choices will not be suitable for everyone. By having a customized Wealth Building Formula tailored to your needs and goals—by understanding your formula and working it properly—you can make the right financial choice for you or at least see what the result of your choice will be.

We've never had two clients whose formulas were exactly the same. No client lives exactly the same way another does. Your formula has to be customized to the way you wish to live, now and in your future. There are some people who, if we said to them, "Don't pay off your mortgage quickly," and showed them how this could get them to their planning goals two or three years faster, might feel comfortable doing so.

There could be another client who tells us, "You know, I can see it would benefit us, but we can't sleep at night with this debt. We have to pay it off." Well, if you can't sleep at night and it's going to cause you stress and anxiety, then pay off that debt quicker; just understand, it means that you're going to work longer and harder in life or take on more risk in your investment portfolio for the cash flow you need. The important lesson here is that you need to know what the effect of a choice is so you can make an *informed* choice. It is up to you.

We equate the Wealth Building Formula to having a physical exam. Suppose you wake up one day with a pain in your chest. You have this pain for days, maybe even for weeks. You try to ignore it, but you can't. What do you do? By this time, you're scared to go to the doctor because he or she might tell you that it's serious.

Ultimately you do go, and the doctor either tells you that it is in fact serious or that it's not. At least knowing what the problem is means that you can make an informed decision about how to proceed. But if you live with the stress and anxiety of the unknown and don't do anything about it, then you don't put yourself in control of the situation.

That's what the Wealth Building Formula does: It allows you to make a series of informed choices to get you to your goal, and it takes away the stress and anxiety of not knowing where you stand.

It Changed Al's Life

Al is an example of this; he saw the power of what having something like the Wealth Building Formula can do for you because of what it did for him. When he started looking at his plan many years ago, his goal was to be independent by the time he was fifty. He made it by forty-eight. It was solely due to the Wealth Building Formula and making informed and better financial choices.

What are some valuable ways for a person to work their Wealth Building Formula? Let's say you are a business owner. Someone makes you a purchase offer for $1 million, and you're eager to accept it. But if you haven't calculated your Wealth Building Formula or don't know what your current cash flow needs are or what kind of wealth you need to have to create that cash flow now and in the future, then you don't know whether or not to make that deal.

If your adviser told you that you'd need to get $2 million for your business to have the cash flow you require now and for the rest of your life, you could then go back to the potential buyer with that number. In the event that they won't go any higher, you can take that offer and also understand what you need to do with the money in order to make up the shortfall between what you have now and what you'll need in the future.

Alternatively, you can take steps to increase the value of your business. Do you raise your prices, cut expenses, hire more people, build a new location, or buy a second business to merge with the first? Knowing the effect these choices will have on your cash flow provides another valuable lesson in working your Wealth Building Formula.

Working your formula means you're doing things with a purpose that's aligned with your plan, not flying blind on a wing and a prayer, hoping that you've made the right financial choice. Starting sooner, as opposed to later, is another critical factor, as we'll discuss in the next chapter on the power of compounding.

Amin's Optional Money Plan Exercise: Boring, Maybe, But Powerful In Practice

At 10:47 p.m., nobody "decides to eat healthy." They *default* to whatever is easiest.

Money works the same way. When you're busy, tired, or distracted, you don't necessarily "choose" your spending; your habits or emotions choose for you.

That's why personal finance takes the same ingredients as fitness: time, attention, patience, and a plan.

Not a strict plan. A usable, realistic one.

A spending plan isn't restriction. It's control. You still have full freedom; this just makes sure your freedom isn't accidentally emotional.

The research backs that up:

- In classic household-wealth research, simply having a plan was associated with roughly a 20 percent higher net worth (and similar increases in gross financial assets).[16] That's not magic; planning changes behavior.
- People with a "spending plan" report feeling more in control (62 percent), more confident (55 percent), and more secure (52 percent) than people without one.[17]

So here's the deal: If I offered you a twenty-five-minute task that reliably increases clarity and reduces financial "mystery months," would you take it?

The Twenty-Five-Minute Setup (Then Five Minutes A Week)

If you want this done cleanly in one place: Download the CakeClub app or a personal finance app that allows you to connect your cards/ accounts, set your spending plan, and let the app keep the scoreboard for you. In about twenty-five minutes, you can go from "I think I'm fine" to "I know exactly what's happening."

- Minute 1–3: Visit and review the app of your choice. Download the app and set up your profile.
- Minute 4–10: Connect your bank accounts and credit cards. Not ready? Add transactions manually for a week.
- Minute 11–15: Review the last seven to fourteen days, fix categories, and make sure the feed looks right.
- Minute 16–20: Choose your spending plan from the choices provided, then add two weekly caps for the categories that drift (food out, shopping, rideshare, entertainment).
- Minute 21–23: Turn on alerts so you get a heads-up before you overspend.
- Minute 24–25: Choose one small change for this week (e.g., two additional dinners at home, one less ride, downgrade one subscription).
- Weekly upkeep (five minutes): Check the dashboard, recategorize anything weird, and adjust one cap.

CakeClub Slices

- Create your personalized Wealth Building Formula
    - Learn the relationship among saving, years you have to work, percent return on your portfolio, and how all affect how much wealth you have and determine the life you will lead now and in the future.
- Work your Wealth Building Formula—take the money exercise
    - Download the CakeClub app or a similar personal finance app and take the twenty-five-minute setup.
    - If you want guided help, try an AI-powered financial assistant to talk through your questions. See the Resources section at the back of the book.

5

The Power Of Compounding

Working Your Wealth Building Formula

My life has been a product of compound interest.
—Warren Buffett, investor and philanthropist

Do you want to make the best-informed financial decision all of the time? First, create your Wealth Building Formula.

Then, understand the principle of compounding. Compound interest is the interest calculated on both the initial principal and the accumulated interest from previous periods, allowing wealth or debt to grow exponentially over time. If you understand and use the principle of compounding along with what we call the "Tax Savings Savings Effect" (explained in the next chapter), you will make the correct financial choice consistently.

Human beings are linear thinkers. For example, if we're taking a trip from New York to San Francisco, we tend to think in terms of straight lines; we don't consider all the twists and turns between here and there.

Humans don't think in terms of complicated formulas; that's why we need calculators, like calculating mortgages.

Money growth doesn't work in a linear fashion either; it can compound in a geometric way. Banks in the nineteenth century used simple interest calculations, but they very rapidly realized that compounding was a far better way to make money. Albert Einstein was also purported to have said, "Those who understand compound interest make it, those who don't, pay it."

Most people don't really understand the power of compounding, and the lack of that knowledge can hinder their ability to make better financial choices. People intellectually comprehend compounding on some level but usually not with any real clarity—or they simply don't believe it.

One good analogy is to think of how bacteria grow in petri dishes. A bacterial colony starts out slowly; one cell becomes two, which become four, and so on. But at a certain point the doubling really takes off, and you're talking about much larger numbers being created in the same span of time. This is sort of how compounding works: It starts slowly. It takes time. But if you're steady with it, it gets to a point where it grows at a much more rapid pace.

With that in mind, let's explore the power of compounding and the "saving now versus later" concept. Let's use two people as examples: the Go-Getter and the Slowpoke. Compounding always rewards the person who saves sooner. As shown in table 1, our Go-Getter has $5,500 to save each year, and she saves it in an IRA (individual retirement account) or a 401(k), so there are no taxes to pay on the earnings. The investments in the account grow 7 percent per year. After ten years, she stops saving and just lets the money in the account grow and the interest earnings compound. Meanwhile, the Slowpoke also has $5,500 coming in, but she finds ways to spend it. She does this for ten years, then starts saving in an IRA.

Table 1: The Power Of Compounding

Savings Now Versus Later

	The Go-Getter		The Slowpoke	
Year	Contribution	Wealth	Contribution	Wealth
1	$5,500	$5,885	$0	$0
2	$5,500	$12,182	$0	$0
3	$5,500	$18,920	$0	$0
4	$5,500	$26,129	$0	$0
5	$5,500	$33,843	$0	$0
6	$5,500	$42,097	$0	$0
7	$5,500	$50,929	$0	$0
8	$5,500	$60,379	$0	$0
9	$5,500	$70,490	$0	$0
10	$5,500	$81,310	$0	$0
11	$0	$87,001	$5,500	$5,885
12	$0	$93,092	$5,500	$12,182
13	$0	$99,608	$5,500	$18,920
14	$0	$106,581	$5,500	$26,129
15	$0	$114,041	$5,500	$33,843
16	$0	$122,024	$5,500	$42,097
17	$0	$130,566	$5,500	$50,929
18	$0	$139,705	$5,500	$60,379
19	$0	$149,485	$5,500	$70,490
20	$0	$159,949	$5,500	$81,310
21	$0	$171,145	$5,500	$92,886
22	$0	$183,125	$5,500	$105,274
23	$0	$195,944	$5,500	$118,528
24	$0	$209,660	$5,500	$132,710
25	$0	$224,336	$5,500	$147,884
26	$0	$240,040	$5,500	$164,121
27	$0	$256,843	$5,500	$181,495
28	$0	$274,822	$5,500	$200,084
29	$0	$294,059	$5,500	$219,975

	The Go-Getter		The Slowpoke	
Year	**Contribution**	**Wealth**	**Contribution**	**Wealth**
30	$0	$314,643	$5,500	$241,258
31	$0	$336,668	$5,500	$264,032
32	$0	$360,235	$5,500	$288,399
33	$0	$385,452	$5,500	$314,472
34	$0	$412,433	$5,500	$342,370
35	$0	$441,303	$5,500	$372,221
36	$0	$472,195	$5,500	$404,161
37	$0	$505,248	$5,500	$438,337
38	$0	$540,616	$5,500	$474,906
39	$0	$578,459	$5,500	$514,034
40	$0	$618,951	$5,500	$555,902
41	$0	$662,277	$5,500	$600,700
42	$0	$708,637	$5,500	$648,634
43	$0	$758,241	$5,500	$699,923
Total Contributions	$55,000		$181,500	

(7 percent assumed rate of return)

By year forty-three, our Go-Getter (who put away $5,500 for those first ten years and then didn't save any more—for a total of $55,000 in contributions) has more money than the Slowpoke (who waited until year eleven and then saved for thirty-three years—for a total of $181,500 in contributions). The Slowpoke saved more than three times the amount of the Go-Getter but was still behind.

The lesson is clear: It takes you longer to create wealth if you don't take advantage of compounding. If you save later, you have to save more, so you work harder and can even end up with less than the person who saves and takes advantage of compounding sooner.

When we show people the chart we've included here, they'll often look at it, shrug, and say, "I'm flat broke! There's no way I will be able to save that much money."

We say, "Yes, that may be true. But you know what? You are still young. Even if you start small, say $100 per month, time is on your side, and the choices you make over the next ten, twenty, or thirty years are going to decide how much more money and how much more wealth you have in the future versus now. You can be the Slowpoke and have less, or you can be the Go-Getter and have more." The rules apply no matter where you are in your life.

You may have difficulty saving $5,500 per year right now. We know we did when we first started saving. Maybe you can only save a little more than $200 per month or $2,750 per year. So, instead of accumulating $758,241 per the illustration above, you will have accumulated half or about $379,120. Not bad.

We don't want to blow your minds, but let's dream a bit big for a minute. Let's say you can save $100,000 per year someday. Then, suppose that you continue to save beyond the tenth year. The Slowpoke never catches up with you, and the gap of wealth between the two of you is just tremendous. See table 2. We just wanted you to see and be inspired by the power of compounding.

The key lesson to harnessing the power of compounding is to save now rather than later. If you're looking at our Integrated Cash Flow Management Approach, that means when you find more investable cash, save it now rather than later.

Table 2: The Power Of Compounding

Savings Now Versus Later—Saving Big

	The Go-Getter		The Slowpoke	
	Savings $100,000/year from year 1		Savings $100,000/year from year 11	
Year	Contribution	Wealth	Contribution	Wealth
1	$100,000	$107,000	$0	$0
2	$100,000	$221,490	$0	$0
3	$100,000	$343,994	$0	$0
4	$100,000	$475,074	$0	$0
5	$100,000	$615,329	$0	$0
6	$100,000	$765,402	$0	$0
7	$100,000	$925,980	$0	$0
8	$100,000	$1,097,799	$0	$0
9	$100,000	$1,281,645	$0	$0
10	$100,000	$1,478,360	$0	$0
11	$100,000	$1,688,845	$100,000	$107,000
12	$100,000	$1,914,064	$100,000	$221,490
13	$100,000	$2,155,049	$100,000	$343,994
14	$100,000	$2,412,902	$100,000	$475,074
15	$100,000	$2,688,805	$100,000	$615,329
16	$100,000	$2,984,022	$100,000	$765,402
17	$100,000	$3,299,903	$100,000	$925,980
18	$100,000	$3,637,896	$100,000	$1,097,799
19	$100,000	$3,999,549	$100,000	$1,281,645
20	$100,000	$4,386,518	$100,000	$1,478,360
21	$100,000	$4,800,574	$100,000	$1,688,845
22	$100,000	$5,243,614	$100,000	$1,914,064
23	$100,000	$5,717,667	$100,000	$2,155,049
24	$100,000	$6,224,904	$100,000	$2,412,902
25	$100,000	$6,767,647	$100,000	$2,688,805
26	$100,000	$7,348,382	$100,000	$2,984,022
27	$100,000	$7,969,769	$100,000	$3,299,903
28	$100,000	$8,634,653	$100,000	$3,637,896
29	$100,000	$9,346,079	$100,000	$3,999,549

	The Go-Getter		The Slowpoke	
	Savings $100,000/year from year 1		Savings $100,000/year from year 11	
Year	Contribution	Wealth	Contribution	Wealth
30	$100,000	$10,107,304	$100,000	$4,386,518
31	$100,000	$10,921,815	$100,000	$4,800,574
32	$100,000	$11,793,343	$100,000	$5,243,614
33	$100,000	$12,725,876	$100,000	$5,717,667
34	$100,000	$13,723,688	$100,000	$6,224,904
35	$100,000	$14,791,346	$100,000	$6,767,647
36	$100,000	$15,933,740	$100,000	$7,348,382
37	$100,000	$17,156,102	$100,000	$7,969,769
38	$100,000	$18,464,029	$100,000	$8,634,653
39	$100,000	$19,863,511	$100,000	$9,346,079
40	$100,000	$21,360,957	$100,000	$10,107,304
41	$100,000	$22,963,224	$100,000	$10,921,815
42	$100,000	$24,677,650	$100,000	$11,793,343
43	$100,000	$26,512,085	$100,000	$12,725,876
Total Contributions	$4,300,000		$3,300,000	

(7 percent assumed rate of return)

The Geometric Jump

Compounding is actually pretty amazing. If you have a plan in mind over ten, twenty, thirty, or forty years, compounding works in a special way we call "geometric compounding." Let's say that a person starting from zero today has a twenty-five-year wealth goal to be independent and calculates the amount of wealth needed to accomplish that (using the Wealth Building Formula).

There is an amount that person must save each year at an assumed rate of return to reach that goal. The key is to get to geometric compounding. Geometric compounding works in a way that's very predictable—you can calculate it very easily—but because compounding starts off slowly and only gains a lot of steam way down the road, it can discourage you from saving or making the proper financial choice.

What do we mean by that? While compounding occurs from when you first begin to save, the real power of compounding occurs in the later stages of your wealth building. If you diligently save what you are supposed to save annually, then you will reach geometric compounding about two-thirds of the way through the time frame of your financial plan. At this point, if you look at what you have accrued in wealth, you will see that you have about one-third of what you need to be financially independent.

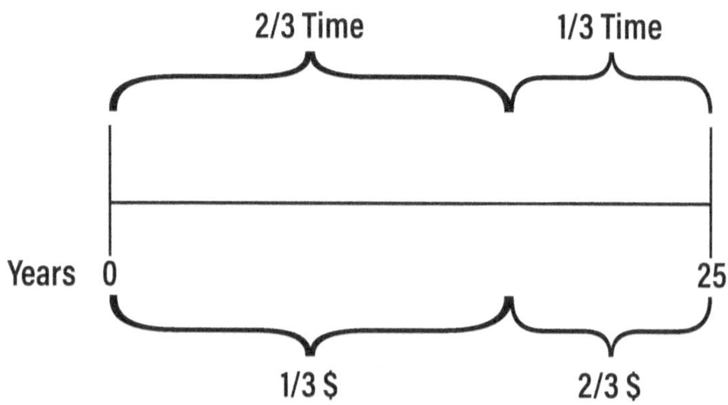

The first two-thirds of the time period, you only accumulate one-third of the dollars of wealth you need. The last one-third of the time, you accumulate two-thirds of the wealth you need.

Imagine—it took you two-thirds of the years in your financial plan to grow only one-third of what you need. Makes you feel good, right? Probably not; if you hired workers to build a new home, and they asked for two-thirds of the money to build one-third of your house, would you agree to that? No, of course not. If you have paid them two-thirds of the money, you want the home project to be two-thirds done.

This is linear thinking. Money and wealth do not grow that way. So, when you see two-thirds of the time pass, and you see only one-third of the wealth goal, you are not happy. You may think, *I have to make up two-thirds of my financial wealth goal, and I have only one-third of my time left.* Again, you may intellectually understand compounding, but emotionally, this does not feel good.

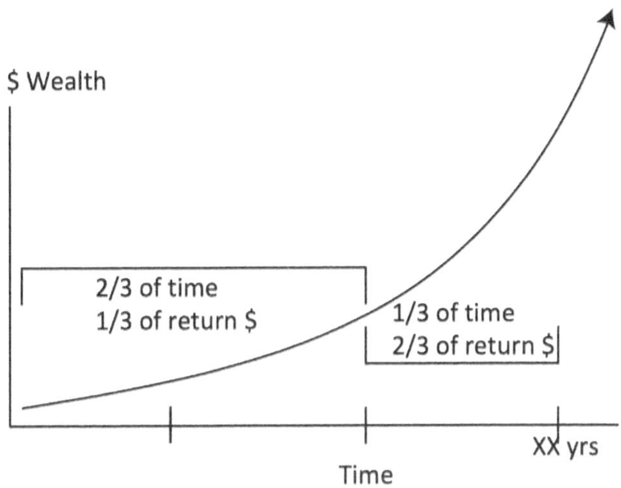

If you have saved faithfully, the "magic" of compounding occurs in the last one-third of the time, generating two-thirds of the returns.

You might think, I am not going to make it. When people think they're not going to make their financial goals, they tend to make poor financial choices. They make decisions like, *I'm not one of the chosen ones, so I might as well just spend and enjoy life.* Or they might decide, *I'm not getting enough return. My uncle knows this really great guy who guarantees a 50 percent rate of return per year. So if I really goose up my rate of return, maybe I can take on more risk and make up for the time that I've lost.*

Folks, if it sounds too good to believe, it probably is. People who throw common sense to the wind and take inordinate risks lose money. If you just give compounding a chance, you will make it.

Stick With The Plan

Even though you're two-thirds through your allotted time and see that you have only saved a third of what you need, stick with it, because the magic of what we call the "geometric jump" happens in that last third of your financial plan. If we were to draw a line showing the progress of geometric compounding, the line would be relatively flat from year zero to about twelve, and then it would go up geometrically.

People often don't understand this, and even when it's explained, they may not believe it. Because of that, they make poor financial choices that prevent them from reaching that geometric jump or compounding adequately in the years they wish.

We worked with a young entrepreneur in Dallas. William's IT consulting company was doing very well, but suddenly cash flow was getting tight. William was in his mid-thirties, had a family, and was looking at college savings for his kids as well as saving for financial freedom sometime in his fifties. All of a sudden, he couldn't save for education, or even contribute to the company 401(k) and pension plan. He was working long hours and was really frustrated by that state of affairs, so he called us in.

Owning a lot of computer-related equipment, his company had about $500,000 in debt. Like most people, he was out to pay this debt down quickly, over about five years or less if he could. But what William was not seeing was that the loan principal payments were hurting the company's cash flow and decreasing his personal cash flow to the extent that he took home less and could not save in his pension plans.

Getting him to renegotiate the debt with the bank to pay it off over fifteen years (the equipment's useful life was up to fifteen years), instead of five, loosened up a lot of cash flow in his company—over $60,000 per year. Now he could start funding his pension plans, save on income taxes through the pension plan deduction, and get back to compounding his wealth and achieving his goals in the time frame he desired.

Another set of clients had a couple of coffee shops in buildings they owned. They were renegotiating debt on these buildings for $2 million to pay off the debt on their other buildings over fifteen years. There were points and other bank fees they were paying that were costing them quite a lot, and they needed help.

In line with our Integrated Cash Flow Management Approach, we said, "How can we find more investable cash?"

We met with the clients and their bankers and explained that we would like either an interest-only loan or a loan that could be amortized over thirty years. In the end, we were able to find investable cash of tens of thousands of dollars per year for our client due to the bank accepting a longer payout time period. They had the choice of putting this cash toward a pension plan (getting more investable cash due to tax savings), using it to expand the business, or using it to help them build more wealth.

At the same time, we were able to renegotiate the fees they were paying on the loan, saving them thousands of additional dollars. Knowing their Wealth Building Formula and employing our Integrated Cash Flow Management Approach enabled them to recognize an opportunity to achieve geometric compounding sooner.

How Do I Start Taking Advantage Of Compounding?

What if you hit a rough patch with your career or in your business? Perhaps you would have to save $10,000 a year to achieve your financial goals, but maybe right now you can only save $5,000 or even less. The key is saving any amount you can, maybe even just fifty to one hundred dollars a month, as soon as possible (saving now versus later) and then targeting to save the rest when you can.

Even if you start out saving $1,000 a year, knowing that you need to save $10,000 or more annually, you will eventually find a way to do that because now you have a target; before, you had none at all. The sooner you begin, the further the power of compounding and getting to geometric compounding will take you.

But what's the best way to save your money while preventing it from being depleted by taxes? We'll discuss that next.

— Application Box —

Amin's 1 Percent Rule (Because Habits Quit When They Hurt)

Most people don't fail at saving because they lack discipline. They fail because they start too big. They try to jump from "zero" to "20 percent," their lifestyle revolts, and the plan dies by Thursday.

Behavioral economics has a simpler take: Don't rely on leftover money or heroic willpower. Make saving automatic and small enough that your brain doesn't fight it. Richard Thaler's blunt point is that people save when it's built into the system, not when they hope something is "left at the end of the month."[18]

Here's the rule:

If you can't save money, start with 1 percent.

Not 20 percent. Not a whimsical number provided to you by some "expert." One percent.

If you bring in $2,000 a month, that's $20 in savings. Maybe you won't feel it. Try it. Or try something smaller at first. That's the point. Start somewhere. You're not trying to get rich on $20. You're training your system to move money *without debate.*

And systems work. When people are put on "save more later" autopilot, saving rates can climb dramatically over time—Thaler and Benartzi's "Save More Tomorrow" approach more than tripled average saving rates (from 3.5 percent to 11.6 percent in twenty-eight months) in an early implementation.[19] Defaults are powerful, too: In classic workplace data, automatic enrollment in the savings plan of the company drove participation to about 86 percent, versus 37 percent for similar-tenure employees who had to opt in.[20]

Translation: small + automatic beats big + painful (emotional).

Amin's Advice: Do It Today (Two Minutes)

1. Calculate 1 percent of your monthly income. Take what you expect to earn this month and multiply by 0.01. If income varies, use last month's deposit total.
2. Move that 1 percent somewhere separate: a savings account, brokerage, cash envelope—anywhere it won't get "accidentally spent."
3. Make it repeat. Set an automatic transfer for the day you get paid (or the next morning).
4. Scale gently. After thirty days, raise it to 2 percent. Then 3 percent. If money is tight, increase by 1 percent every two months instead.

That's it.

You're not proving you're perfect. You're proving you can keep a promise to yourself—small, automatic, and unstoppable.

CakeClub Slices

- Be a "Go-Getter" to take advantage of the power of compounding—prioritize saving cash flow now and get to the geometric jump.
- Getting to geometric compounding takes time: Patience brings great rewards.
- Start saving 1 percent or whatever works for you. Don't make saving painful.

6

The Tax Savings Savings Effect

More Working Your Wealth Building Formula

You don't pay taxes; they take taxes.
—Chris Rock, actor and comedian

The financial services giant Morgan Stanley once ran an advertisement that said: "You must pay taxes. But there's no law that says you gotta leave a tip."

A key component to working your personal Wealth Building Formula is understanding how the "Tax Savings Savings Effect" works. This is another way to find more investable cash or cash flow through our Integrated Cash Flow Management Approach, which allows you to save more money without working harder or longer.

Going back to the Wealth Building Formula, if people have to save $10,000 a year and are able to do so, then they're going to be on track for the time frame in which they want to be independent. However, if we can find more investable cash and they decide to save that too, they'll get to their wealth-building goal sooner, or have more wealth when they get there, or can reduce the risk of their portfolio. So how do we accomplish that?

Say that you have $5,000 to $10,000 put away, but because of various expenses, you can't save any more than $5,000 per year. You know that you have to save $10,000 a year to achieve your financial goals, but the only option you seem to have to achieve that is to work harder at your job.

Assume that if you work harder in your business or for your employer, you could earn $3,000 more. At this point, you say, "I can save this additional $3,000. I'm going to put it in my savings account," and you're pleased because you feel that you've come close to your annual goal.

But have you? Between state and federal taxes, it's not hard to wind up in a 40 percent tax bracket. You just earned another $3,000, and 40 percent of that is $1,200, meaning that you have to come up with $1,200 in extra cash just to pay your taxes. You want to save at least the $3,000, but in order to pay your income taxes you would have to subtract $1,200 from the $3,000.

Once you realize this, the question becomes, "How can I make up that missing $1,200?" The obvious choice is to work harder to make even more to cover that savings shortfall. So you decide to work harder and make that additional $1,200.

But now you have to pay 40 percent of that new $1,200—it is earned income—so you are still short of that elusive goal. You're getting closer, but it seems as though no matter how much work you pile on, that 40 percent tax bite undoes your efforts.

Table 3: Tax Savings Savings Effect
(Or How To Turn $3,000 Into $5,000 Without Working Harder)

$3,000 x 40 percent	=	$1,200
$1,200 x 40 percent	=	$480
$480 x 40 percent	=	$192
$192 x 40 percent	=	$76.80
$76.80 x 40 percent	=	$30.72
$30.72 x 40 percent	=	$12.29
$12.29 x 40 percent	=	$4.92
$4.92 x 40 percent	=	$1.97
$1.97 x 40 percent	=	$0.79
$0.79 x 40 percent	=	$0.32
$0.32 x 40 percent	=	$0.13
$0.13 x 40 percent	=	$0.05
$0.05 x 40 percent	=	$0.02
Total (rounded) $5,000 x 40 percent	=	$2,000

So, to save $3,000 (non–tax sheltered), you must earn $5,000 and pay $2,000 in income taxes.

Having to earn $5,000 to net $3,000 after tax makes sense since 40 percent of $5,000 equals taxes of $2,000.

The Tax Savings Savings Effect

If you begin to save the $3,000 in a tax-sheltered way (e.g., a 401(k)) you reduce income taxes. If you save those tax savings, you can reverse the above and save $5,000 by initially saving $3,000.

The more money you earn, the more taxes you're going to pay. This is the tax effect. Per table 3, you can see that you'll actually have to earn

$5,000 to have that full $3,000 to save, because if you earn $5,000 and are in a 40 percent tax bracket, your taxes on that will be $2,000.

But There's Good News

You can make taxes work for you, instead of against you, if you utilize the Tax Savings Savings Effect. Finding tax savings and then saving the investable cash from that tax savings has a big compounding effect on your wealth.

Let's say you find a way to shelter your $3,000 from taxes so that you can make (or beat) your savings goal. One way is to contribute the extra earnings to a pension plan. Sheltering those earnings in a pension plan turns them from a tax liability into a tax deduction. The $3,000 is now subtracted from your taxable income rather than included in it. If you're earning $50,000 and you put this $3,000 into a pension plan, your taxable income is now only $47,000.

So now, if you're saving taxes on 40 percent of $3,000, there's now $1,200 in taxes you effectively won't have to pay: Either the government will refund you $1,200, or you can reduce your withholdings or quarterly tax payments by $1,200.

You now have $1,200 of "found money." You can either spend it or save it. If you save it, you will get to your financial goals sooner, have more cash flow or wealth when you get there, or reduce the risk in your portfolio.

The better financial choice is to take the $1,200 and also contribute that to your pension plan. If you save that money in your pension plan, you save 40 percent of $1,200 due to the tax deduction, which is $480. You can contribute that $480 to the pension plan, and you save 40 percent of that, which is $192.

Any person who begins saving $3,000 a year can actually save $5,000 a year if they save the tax savings that they were going to pay to the government. Let's add another zero (we know it is much higher and maybe you won't be able to afford it). If you can save $30,000 into a tax-sheltered pension plan, you can save $50,000 due to the Tax Savings Savings Effect.

Two young partners at a Midwest law firm we consulted with were able to save $50,000 a year in their particular pension plan due to this strategy. You can imagine the cash flow effect they got from that: The government was paying for almost half of their pension contribution!

Recently, dealing with two young physician practice partners, in examining their business, we were able to show them a pension plan where they could contribute almost $100,000 per year and save almost $50,000 in federal and state income taxes. For them, they could shelter almost $100,000 to grow tax deferred, have the government pay about half of it, and have a net cost of $50,000 to fund pensions for their employees. This is the power of the Tax Savings Savings Effect.

Understanding the Tax Savings Savings Effect allows you to work your Wealth Building Formula and, along with the power of compounding, to make the 100 percent correct financial choice to save more money without working one day longer.

The Key Word Is "Smarter"

Keep in mind that the power of understanding all of the concepts we have discussed so far is what we mean by the word *smarter* in "make smarter financial choices that don't require you to work harder or longer." Just by doing what we call "shuffling paper"—simply filling out paperwork—you can utilize compounding and the Tax Savings Savings Effect to your advantage to grow your wealth in less time and with less work.

Life insurance can be another example: We had a business client who was paying a life insurance premium of $10,000, which is not a tax-deductible item; thus, because of the tax bite (assuming a 40 percent tax bracket), he actually had to earn $16,667 (40 percent of $16,667 equals $6,667 that would go to income tax) to get that $10,000 for the premium.

Suppose you could find a policy that protects you the same way but only costs you $4,000? Your savings before taxes is $6,000 ($10,000 less $4,000). Using the Tax Savings Savings Effect illustration and assuming you could place the $6,000 (and the tax savings on it) in a pension, your total savings after taxes is now $10,000. That means that with the same $10,000, if you could structure it this way, you could actually pay for your insurance for free and save the $10,000 per year.

When we talked about mortgages, we've only discussed the compounding effect: If you could pay less on your mortgage by having an interest-only mortgage or a longer payout, you could save that money, have it compound, and get to your wealth goals sooner. But there's something else to consider when you look at compounding: the Tax Savings Savings Effect.

Remember the example where you had $3,000 a year to save? Let's say that when you earned it, instead of saving it in your pension plan, you took the $3,000 and paid down more principal on your mortgage. When you earn this $3,000, you have to pay tax on it. When you contribute the $3,000 to a pension, it becomes a tax deduction and you do not pay tax on it.

Because paying mortgage principal is not a tax deduction, in paying the $3,000 toward the principal of the mortgage instead of contributing to your pension, you have to pay $2,000 in taxes. This means that every time you pay principal of $3,000 on your mortgage, you have to go out and actually earn $5,000—$2,000 to pay your taxes and $3,000 to pay the bank. If you do this, you put yourself in the position of paying more in taxes, which takes away from your *C* (investable cash) and means taking more time to get to geometric compounding.

The savvy way to use the compounding and Tax Savings Savings Effect in that example is to take that $3,000, contribute this amount to your pension plan, and save the tax savings of $2,000 or a total of $5,000 per year.

How many people do you know who pay extra on their mortgage each month? Doing this blindly is what we call being "anti-geometric." If you fail to use the power of compounding or of the Tax Savings Savings Effect, you can wind up having less wealth and thus less cash flow; having to earn more money in your investment portfolio during the life of your portfolio, thereby having to increase risk; or having to work longer or harder.

How To Make It Work In Your Favor

"All right, I found all this extra investable cash. How can I use compounding and tax savings to the maximum?"

There's a priority regarding where you're going to save money, and the first priority is trying to get the most compounding you can. Normally, you do this by putting it in the most tax-sheltered, tax-advantageous account you can. That means putting your investable cash savings in a tax-advantaged or tax-shelter account where not only are you getting a tax deduction, but the money also is growing tax deferred, you're not paying tax on the earnings. That account could be a savings plan like a 401(k), which is also called a *defined contribution plan*; a pension plan or deferred compensation plan at work; or, if you have a business, a 401(k), a cash balance plan, or a *defined benefit plan*. Any of these would be your first and best choices.

If you can't put your money where you can receive a tax deduction, the second choice is to put it into an account which may be tax deductible and will at least be growing tax-deferred, like a traditional or Roth IRA or maybe some sort of insurance vehicle.

A side note on IRAs: As you grow older, you may get to a point when you can have these IRAs rolled over into a Roth IRA. A Roth IRA allows you to take out these monies tax-free in the future or to pass them on to the next generation, who may not have to pay the tax on the earnings. It's not as advantageous as the first choice—your 401(k) or pension plan—but it's a good second choice if it's what's available to you.

The last choice is to put your savings into a taxable account. This is just a bank account or an investment account that offers you no tax advantage. You've already paid the taxes on this money, and you will pay the tax on the earnings. People normally save in all three categories: tax-advantaged, tax-deferred, and taxable accounts.

Another place to put money is in real estate. You can buy real estate and get a mortgage on it. As it grows in value, that value (equity) will grow tax-deferred. You're only going to pay taxes on it when you sell it. When that real estate is sold, you get another tax advantage called capital gains treatment, which is normally taxed at a lower percentage than ordinary income. Another nice aspect of real estate is that sometimes, if you're purchasing it through corporations or other entities, you can get tax deductions that help to shelter other income.

Another great option with real estate investment is that you can take money from the equity you have built by borrowing from it. You don't pay taxes on this. This can allow you to take advantage of compounding and the Tax Savings Savings Effect.

Sophie was a thirty-five-year-old manager in a Fortune 500 company; she had a net worth of $500,000, which was in two pieces of real estate. Her primary residence was a small apartment in Florida, so she did not pay state income taxes. She inherited another small apartment in the same area from her parents, which she rented out. Both properties were debt-free.

Trying to save more to grow more wealth, she came to us and said, "I need to bolster my cash flow, and while I get some rental income, I don't know how to generate more cash flow without selling one or both of the properties, which I don't really want to do."

Because Sophie had previously created a financial plan with us, we knew her Wealth Building Formula and made this recommendation to her: "You have $500,000 of real estate, which you own outright. Given today's low-interest-rate environment, why don't you borrow $250,000 from your combined real estate, which is about half of what its value is? In effect, you're borrowing this at about a 4 percent rate, and you've been earning 7 percent or more on your portfolio. If you take this $250,000 out and put it into your portfolio, you will earn the difference between the 7 percent you've been earning on average and the 4 percent that you're paying on the mortgage—so you will net an extra 3 percent."

Seven percent of $250,000 equals $17,500, so Sophie was going to increase her cash flow by $17,500. As shown in table 4, she was going to increase her net cash flow after interest and taxes by $6,250 per year—not by working harder, not by going back to work, just by "shuffling paper." Even on an after-tax basis she actually made out even better than that because she was able to deduct the interest for that mortgage on her tax return.

Table 4: Leveraging The Equity In Your Home To Create Investable Cash

Take out a $250,000 mortgage at 4 percent, invest it for returns of 7 percent.

Cash In		
	$17,500	Income earned from investing
Less	$5,250	Income taxes on the income (blended cap gains and ordinary rates)
Net Income	$12,250	
Cash Out		
	$10,000	4 percent interest on $250,000 mortgage
Less	$4,000	Possible tax savings on deducting interest ($10,000 x 40 percent)
Net Cost	$6,000	
Net Cash Flow Found		
	$6,250	Possible net investable cash created
	$10,417	If saved in a 401(k) and saved the tax savings

Again, just by using the Tax Savings Savings Effect and compounding, we were able to come up with a solution that allowed her to increase her cash flow without working one day longer.

You might say, "She had to pay tax on the amount of earnings she had in her portfolio," and that's true. But there are strategies that we'll discuss later that mean you don't have to pay the full tax rate on the amount you're earning on investments. She could have sold one of her homes. Let's say one of her homes was worth that $250,000; she could have sold the home and paid taxes on the gains. But by borrowing the $250,000, she did not have a taxable event. She could actually take that money from the real estate, not pay any taxes on it, invest it, and find more cash flow to grow more wealth, again, without working one day longer. An added benefit, she gets to see the value of the properties rise, too, adding to her wealth.

Why "More Income" Isn't Necessarily The Full Answer

Income matters. But management matters just as much, because management is what turns money into stability, control, and possibly less stress.

The Consumer Financial Protection Bureau (CFPB) describes financial well-being in practical terms: having control over day-to-day finances, the capacity to absorb a shock, and the freedom to make choices that let you enjoy life.[21] Notice what's missing: shame. Financial well-being isn't "never spending." It's not being at war with your own bank account.

Money doesn't automatically create peace. Systems create peace. A sudden pile of cash without a system often just amplifies whatever habits were already running the show.

The Bandwidth Tax

If money stress makes you feel foggy, impatient, or weirdly exhausted, that's not you being dramatic. That's your brain doing math with one eye closed.

Scarcity doesn't just mean "less money." It also means less mental room. Researchers have shown that when people are preoccupied with financial concerns, cognitive performance drops—one widely cited set of experiments found the effect was comparable to about a thirteen-point hit to IQ or the loss of a full night of sleep.[22]

So when someone says, "I can't focus," or "I keep making dumb money choices," the real translation is often: "My bandwidth is being taxed."

And you're not alone. The American Psychological Association reported that 72 percent of Americans said they felt stressed about money at least some time during the past month.[23] That stress doesn't stay politely inside your wallet. It shows up in your attention, your patience, and your relationships. Research on family financial strain finds that economic pressure can ripple into family processes like distress and harsher interactions—because stress changes how people show up.[24]

Make money less emotional by making it more visible.

If money has been making you sharper in the worst way—shorter fuse, shorter focus, shorter horizon—that's not a character flaw. That's the bandwidth tax.

And the fix is not guilt. The fix is control.

When someone feels more in control of their money, they often show up as a calmer version of themselves, more patient, more present, less reactive, because their brain isn't constantly trying to solve a mystery called "Where did it go?"

That's why tools exist: to turn chaos into clarity. Whether you use a notebook, a spreadsheet, or an app that pulls your accounts and cards into one view and categorizes spending for you, the goal is the same: Make money less emotional by making it more visible.

If that visibility helps even one person breathe easier, if it helps a parent be a little more patient, or helps someone stop fearing their bank app like it's a horror movie, that's a real win. And just maybe, knowledge of the Tax Savings Savings Effect will give you another way to control your cash flow.

CakeClub Slices

- Understanding and using the Tax Savings Savings Effect is another way to work your Wealth Building Formula.
- Applying the Tax Savings Savings Effect will help you make better financial decisions, live the life you want now, and achieve your financial goals in the time frame you want.
- Applying the Tax Savings Savings Effect will allow you to find more cash flow to save or spend.
- While "more income" isn't necessarily the full answer, finding more cash flow using the Tax Savings Savings Effect in a smarter way can help to give you more control and reduce stress and anxiety without working one day longer.

7

Finding More Investable Cash

Imagination

Logic will take you from A to B.
Imagination will take you everywhere.
—Albert Einstein, theoretical physicist

Gen Z is finding adulthood more expensive than expected. Facing this, nearly three-quarters of them are taking action to improve their financial health, according to Bank of America's 2025 Better Money Habits report.[25]

"Gen Z is challenging the stereotype when it comes to young people and their finances," said Holly O'Neill, president of consumer, retail, and preferred banking at Bank of America. "Even though they're facing economic barriers and high everyday costs, they are working hard to become financially independent and take control of their money."[26]

Key findings from the study include:

- Over the last twelve months, 72 percent took steps to improve their financial health, such as putting money toward savings (51 percent) or paying down debt (24 percent).
- Nearly two-thirds (64 percent) focused on reducing expenses—41 percent cut back on dining out and 23 percent shopped at more affordable grocery stores.
- And more are going it alone. While 39 percent receive financial support from parents and other family members, this is down from 46 percent a year ago. And they are getting less money—22 percent receive $1,000 or more per month compared to 32 percent a year ago, and 54 percent receive less than $500 per month compared to 44 percent a year ago.
- When it comes to their romantic lives, many Gen Z aren't spending money on dates—with roughly half of men (53 percent) and women (54 percent) spending $0 a month, and 25 percent of men and 30 percent of women spending less than $100 per month.

According to the study, about half (51 percent) of Gen Z surveyed say the high cost of living is a barrier to financial success. Total monthly spending is higher than they thought it would be for 35 percent, especially for everyday expenses, including groceries (63 percent), rent and utilities (47 percent), and dining out (42 percent).[27]

Can you relate to this study? How do you envision the life you want for yourself, now and in the future? Maybe you want to have great vacations, a nice vacation home, or to be able to travel by private jet someday. If you're unable to live the way you wish, no matter how much you're saving toward financial independence, it makes that saving a much harder chore. People want to have choices as to whether they continue to work or to do something else. We at CakeClub believe that they should.

Our Integrated Cash Flow Management Approach, coupled with our Wealth Building Formula process, maps a clear path to achieving these life goals. It's the same for companies and your personal finances: The better financial choices you make, the more you're going to have now and for life. Poor choices will sentence you to working harder in life or not having the options you want.

What Are Your Benchmarks?

We've discussed the process and methodology for making smart choices, and the fact that so many people lack the know-how or tools that businesses use to make those good financial decisions for themselves. Businesses have benchmarks that can be compared to other companies in the same industry.

Most individuals don't have these benchmarks. The most they can do is to look at how much they have in the bank or their investment accounts or if their investments did better than the S&P 500 for the last quarter or year. But they don't know how to bring it all together. They don't have a road map to tell them where they are or a whole view of their finances like a well-run company would.

We've talked through the principle of compounding as a key to achieving your Wealth Building Formula, which says that if you save now rather than later, you're going to have more. If you wait to save until later, you're going to have less wealth and cash flow.

Harnessing the power of compounding sounds simple, but many people just don't do it. Most decisions they make are meant to save later rather than now, because while they intellectually understand compounding, emotionally they don't believe it. People think linearly, and compounding is a geometric calculation.

We've also discussed another thing critical to your Wealth Building Formula, which is understanding the Tax Savings Savings Effect—making the right choices around taxes and finding more investable cash by paying less to the government.

So what does all this mean? When you make uninformed financial decisions, whether it's because you're in a hurry or you don't really understand the ramifications, you can wind up creating a sort of financial domino effect that affects you in ways you don't foresee and eventually leads to you having less cash flow than you need.

We chose to start CakeClub because we wanted to transform lives in the way that having this knowledge transformed ours. As a baker's son, Al had grown up in a profession in which most people worked until they were seventy or older. He saw that he could help other people make better financial choices so they could have the same thing that he eventually achieved: to be financially independent by age forty-eight and be able to do whatever he wished in life beyond that.

Every decision that you make in your financial life—whether it's going out to dinner, subscribing to a streaming service, deciding to buy an insurance policy, buying or leasing a car, paying down a mortgage faster, hiring more employees, expanding your operation, buying another business, or buying more equipment—is going to have an effect on your Wealth Building Formula, your current and future cash flow, and the way you will live now and in the future.

Let's say you make a decision that increases your cash flow, and you decide to save the excess cash flow. You can get to your wealth goals quicker, add more wealth when you get there, or reduce the risk in your investment portfolio. Of those three choices, what we observe that most people find the most attractive among them is "getting to your wealth goals quicker" or what we refer to as "saving years of life."

Saving Years Of Life

You may not have enough wealth to be financially independent right now, but you may have some. We've seen many a well-off person mess up with the wealth they have. They'll be enjoying a smooth sail on the fair winds of a healthy economy, and then suddenly, they get swamped by a big wave. The market tanks, the real estate environment changes, their business is out of sync, or maybe their employer lets them go. Without warning and even though they have some wherewithal, they're not going to have enough to live the life they wish, now or in the future.

When we offer people the options of becoming financially independent sooner, having more wealth when they get there, or reducing the risk in their portfolio, most people say, "I'd like to retire sooner," or "I'd like to be independent sooner." That said, it's our observation that well over 90 percent of the people we've dealt with do not stop working and play golf for the rest of their lives. The vast majority continue to work because they like what they do, hold onto their business because they like their business, or have a life of purpose.

For example, we had a client, Sally, who owned a couple of restaurants and had done very well. She had just turned fifty, and now sixty didn't look that far off. Did she really want to keep working after sixty?

We sat down together and went through a comprehensive personal financial plan with her that encompassed what she wanted in life, what her cash flow was, and all the things we've talked about in earlier chapters. We made sure that she had her own customized Wealth Building Formula.

All she really wanted to know was whether she was going to be OK to retire by the time she was sixty or sixty-five. She was living a pretty good lifestyle; she wanted to get a second home and travel more, but she wasn't sure she could afford that. But it was more important for her to know that, somewhere along the way, she was going to have options and not have to work.

We said, "Sally, we don't think that you're going to have a problem retiring by sixty-five. If you sell your business at the price you need, you could retire closer to sixty."

She said she wanted to live a better lifestyle now rather than later. So we dug into ways that we could improve her cash flow, and we showed her that not only could she have that vacation home now, but that it was very possible for her to be financially independent years earlier than age sixty. Sometimes, by using your imagination and partnering with someone, you can find the answers. One of the problems is that many people do not take the time to ponder, explore, or create with their trusted adviser.

Sally is now in her sixties and still owns her restaurants—although by about age fifty-seven, she no longer needed to work. Realizing that she didn't have to work changed her whole view about the stress and anxiety of running a business. Suddenly, without the pressure, it became more enjoyable to her—more like a game. She was eager to take risks and try new experiences she wouldn't have considered before. She even started a foundation.

That's the power of having a plan and taking the time to work on the business, not just in the business.

One client couple we worked with, Bob and Carol, were both young executives. In the course of sitting down with them, they revealed that although they both liked their careers, they were each interested in doing something different with their lives.

Bob confided that he'd always wanted to be a writer of science fiction. He wanted to take writing courses and see if he could turn out some short stories or a book, but the time demands of his career made that impossible.

Carol wanted to be more active in the community and turn her talents to volunteering or to teaching underprivileged children, particularly those with special needs.

Bob and Carol were in their mid-thirties when they came to see us; they're presently in their mid-forties, and thanks to their dedication to working their Wealth Building Formula, they're within a couple of years of achieving their respective goals.

Use your imagination. Dream of the life you want. Then find out how to make better financial choices and become fully aware of the impact those choices will have on your financial well-being. That's the path to making those dreams your reality: making a conscious choice.

Choose On Purpose, Not By Default

Among our clients was a gentleman who had a strong desire to fund a scholarship. He could have retired sooner had he chosen to invest the $5,000 per year that he was putting toward funding this scholarship, but as he told me, "I would prefer to take my time and to take a little longer to get to retirement, but to also know I could make a difference along the way." People want to be able to make prudent financial decisions, to achieve certain things or options in their life, and also to live the way they want to along the way.

Most people do want to save time, though. By finding additional investable cash, you're saving years of life—years in which you would otherwise have had to work. You get to your options sooner rather than later.

Because they don't have a clear way in which to make a better choice, however, many people make decisions that mean getting to their goals will take longer, or that they'll fail to amass the wealth or the cash flow that they need.

Remember, every financial choice, no matter how small, can have a big impact on your ability to get where you want to go sooner. No financial option exists in a vacuum, and that certainly includes decisions about debt, which we'll cover in depth in the next chapter.

— Application Box —
Amin's Microleaks And The Subscription Mirage

Most "money problems" aren't one big fire. They're a slow leak you stop noticing—because your brain is excellent at ignoring small, repeated pain.

Richard Thaler, a Nobel Laureate behavioral economist, calls this "mental accounting": We sort money into invisible folders, and those folders change how we feel about spending.[28] A $1,200 bill feels like a major event. It triggers attention, comparison, and a decision. But twelve $100 charges often get filed as "small stuff," so they slide past your mental security system.

Subscriptions quietly exploit three predictable quirks:

- Small monthly numbers stay below your "this matters" threshold. When researchers asked people what they spend on subscriptions, the average estimate was $86 per month. When people itemized their actual subscriptions, the average was $219 per month, more than 2.5 times higher.[29]
- Autopay separates the pleasure from the payment. You enjoy the service on Tuesday, but the money leaves your account on a random Thursday while you're living your life. That's not budgeting, it's background radiation.
- Free trials create "I might need this" attachment. Once something is in your routine, canceling feels like losing an option, even if you barely use it. So you keep paying for the possibility.

Here's the uncomfortable part: One survey summary found that 42 percent of people were still paying for a subscription they had forgotten about.[30] That is not a spending choice. That is a subscription choosing *you.*

The Business Rule For Subscriptions

Treat every subscription like an employee on payroll. It must do at least one job:

- save time that you actually use
- improve your health in ways you can feel
- grow income or skills
- reduce stress in a real way
- create joy you use weekly

If it doesn't do a job, it doesn't stay.

The One Habit That Changes Everything: Annualize

Your brain underestimates monthly numbers. So stop speaking "monthly" to yourself.

Every subscription must be expressed in one language: annual cost.

Five "only $15" subscriptions isn't $15. It's $900 per year. And $900 per year is not "petty cash." It's real investable cash (*C*) in your Wealth Building Formula.

The Compounding Reality (Simple, Not Preachy)

If you find *$200 per month* in microleaks and redirect it into a long-term bucket, even a modest market-like return can turn that into hundreds of thousands of dollars over a few decades without you working one day longer. For example: $200 per month invested for approximately forty years at 7 percent grows to roughly $528,000, not guaranteed, just math. That's not "retirement." Those are the options: time, flexibility, and fewer panic decisions.

Amin's Microleak Move Exercise

Do one thing today: Cancel (or downgrade) one subscription, and immediately move that exact monthly amount into your wealth bucket.

Same day. Same dollars.

That last step matters because it turns a "no" into visible progress. You don't just stop spending. You reassign cash flow.

Subscriptions win when they stay invisible. You win when you make them show their work.

CakeClub Slices

- There could be a lot more free cash flow in your spending than you think.
- Finding cash savings also potentially saves years of "having to go to work."
- Perform the "microleak move exercise" and find some cash flow now.

8

Using Debt Smarter

The Truth About Debt And Wealth Creation

Opportunities multiply as they are seized.
—Sun Tzu, Chinese general,
author of *The Art of War*

Generation Z is entering adulthood with more financial burdens than any previous generation, according to one survey.

A poll by Talker Research in 2024 for *Newsweek* revealed that Gen Z—born between 1997 and 2012—carries the highest average personal debt when compared to older counterparts. Their average personal debt is $94,101—far above millennials ($59,181) and Gen X ($53,255).

The data reflects a troubling reality: Younger adults are struggling under the weight of financial pressures. More than half, 52 percent, of Gen Z respondents said debt is on their minds most or all of the time, making it hard to have worry-free moments.

Economic reports, including findings from the New York Federal Reserve, confirm that Gen Z is falling behind on debt payments at increasing rates, with delinquencies greater than ninety days at their highest level in three years.[31]

Obviously, debt is something many young adults may lose sleep over. But would it surprise you to learn there is some debt you should embrace?

Debt Fear Never Sleeps

We've talked a little about how, in our experience, most people fear debt; they've absorbed the teachings of their parents and grandparents or the influencers who say that when you get a chance to pay off debt, you want to do that first, as quickly as possible, and *then* save. Certainly, they say, by the time you reach your retirement years, you want the house paid off and no debt hanging over your head.

People say these things because most people feel really good about the idea of being debt-free. There's an emotional kick to knowing that you don't owe anyone anything, so people take that emotion and equate it with success. It becomes a yardstick: "How can I go into retirement with a mortgage? I'm not successful if I couldn't pay off my debt, right?"

People are obsessed with this, and the root source of that anxiety isn't hard to identify if you have even a nodding acquaintance with twentieth-century history: the Great Depression.

The Grapes Of Wrath Mindset

Many of us have either grandparents or great-grandparents who lived through the Great Depression. The Great Depression scarred anyone who came through it. It was a time in which people lost their homes, jobs, businesses, and dignity.

Al's father was in his early teens during the Great Depression, and he told Al horror stories. Al's grandfather lost his bakery in the Midwest because of the Great Depression. Al's father, at five years old, remembered waking up every day to find his father, who'd been up since dawn, mixing dough and frying doughnuts in a cauldron of boiling fat on the stove of their kitchen. Al's father would help him put the doughnuts on paper on the floor to cool, and then they would sugar the doughnuts. They'd put them in paper containers, and Al's father, aunts, and uncles would go door to door, selling them for a few cents each.

Al's father remembers graduating from eighth grade in bare feet. Until the day he died, whenever Al's father told that story, it was with such searing emotion and such raw hurt that you could almost feel like you were that little boy whose graduation day was stained with the shame and embarrassment of not having shoes.

Al's grandfather could not keep up with the rent; Al's father remembered the day that the landlord came to the door of the house they were renting and told them that they had to get out, right then. They couldn't take their belongings; all they could do was to get in their car and drive away. They had to leave everything behind: their clothes, their furniture—Al's father even had to leave his dog behind, another event that scarred his memory forever. They made their way to the East Coast, to Philadelphia, where eventually they got back on their feet.

Al's father certainly believed that debt was bad, and he never wanted to owe anyone anything. If he couldn't pay cash for something, he didn't buy it. He only bought used cars for cash, and he would never get loans. He never had a credit card. Only one time did he have a mortgage, when, as a young man, he owned a small row home in Philadelphia. The mortgage payment was less than $40 per month. Yet he fell behind on some payments and had to sell the house. He rented forever after. Debt was bad.

Experiences like these, all too common during the Great Depression and during tough financial times, gave birth to what we call "*The Grapes of Wrath* mentality." *The Grapes of Wrath* was a 1940 movie based on a Pulitzer Prize-winning novel by John Steinbeck, directed by Oscar-winning John Ford, and starring Henry Fonda, about the hardships many endured during the Depression.

It's linked to what happened in the Midwest farming belt, but it misled audiences, especially about debt. Being only a generation or two from their pioneer ancestors, most farmers had little or no debt on their farms. Then a great drought created the Dust Bowl. Many farmers that had small amounts of debt due to borrowing for seed or no debt at all. But they couldn't pay this little debt or their property taxes, and lost their farms. Ironically, those farmers who had more debt but also more savings did fine. They had the reserves to weather the downturn. Farmers who did not lost their properties.

It wasn't only the Depression that created hardship and loss; one bank president told us a story about some rental houses his family had owned during World War II. They didn't have any debt on the houses, but because it was wartime, the government set rent limits on them and set them very low. The rents weren't sufficient to cover his parents' costs in upkeep or property taxes, and they eventually had to give away the properties. His parents didn't have the wealth to send him to college, and he had to work his way through school. Why? In part because his parents didn't have the cash reserves to weather the downturn and retain their wealth.

We are telling you these stories to establish the way in which we think about debt and why we think that way. We are told stories about past generations losing property or having financial difficulty, and we associate that with debt: If only they had not had that debt, they would have been OK. But if they had maintained some level of debt to have reserves when times were bad, like a well-run company, they most likely would have been all right. The lesson to be learned here is about using debt smarter.

To pay off debt principal, you must earn money. When you earn money, you have to pay taxes on it. When you pay those taxes, you have to earn more than what you pay to the bank or mortgage company for your debt, so you have to work harder to do that (the Tax Savings Savings Effect). Because of the way tax laws are structured, paying down debt faster means losing the interest deduction sooner. Thus you find yourself paying more taxes now and end up having to wait later to save money, losing the advantage of compounding and the Tax Savings Savings Effect.

During a white-collar recession the US experienced in the late 1980s, many companies had to lay off a lot of their management or white-collar workers. AT&T had a very large operation in our local area, and they too laid off a lot of executives. Many of these executives came to us for advice.

These were people who were accustomed to being able to afford a nice life. They had homes in the area that were very expensive. Most of them were probably in their late forties. They had built up their lifestyle to match their salary in a way that left little room for savings. They hadn't expected to get laid off, and suddenly they were faced with maintaining an expensive lifestyle without the resources to do so.

They did have some savings in their 401(k)s and some stock options (which were now worth less), but they had very little outside of those assets that they could draw on to support them. Most of them had small or no mortgages; they had paid them off quickly but had not saved reserves. Having little or no income, some paid their mortgage payments from their 401(k)s until there was little or nothing left.

Once they exhausted their 401(k)s, what happened? They had to sell their homes at fire-sale prices.

Be Prepared For The Worst, And It Won't Be As Bad

We could help these executives to a certain degree, but the best advice we would give you is to avoid putting yourself in that position in the first place. Start planning well ahead of time for a potential recession or job loss.

As shown in figure 4, suppose that there were two people, each of whom has $500,000 in investments. Each of them buys a house for $500,000.

One of these people hates debt, so he sells his $500,000 in investments and pays off his mortgage. He now owns the house free and clear.

The other homebuyer asks for our advice, and we recommend to her, "Take out a mortgage for as much as possible to preserve the cash you have in your investment account. You will have this money in the event of an emergency, it will continue to grow wealth by compounding, and you will receive extra investable cash by having the mortgage interest as a tax deduction." She put down $100,000 on the house and takes out a $400,000 mortgage, leaving $400,000 in her investment accounts.

Let's further assume that both of these people suddenly lose their jobs, in a recession that strikes right after buying the houses. What choices do each have?

He has a half-million-dollar house he owns free and clear, and she has a $400,000 mortgage and $400,000 in investments.

They're both talented executives, so they're likely to get jobs at some point in the future. But in a down cycle of the economy, it might take a long time to find a new job, or they may have to relocate to find employment. The process may take six months, a year, or even longer.

The person who had the paid-off, free-and-clear house had made what he felt was a safe and wise choice. But now he doesn't have any cash flow coming in. He still has to feed his family and pay for heat, light, home insurance, and property taxes. What options does a person with a half-million-dollar house and no other assets have? He may go to the bank and ask for a home equity loan, but because he has no cash flow, no job, and no liquid assets, he will not get it.

Another option might be to put his house on the market in hopes of a fast sale, which may mean that he'll have difficulty selling it for the price he wants. A recession is the worst time to sell your house because other people may be in the same boat, which means that a lot of people could be flooding the market with homes. But our debt-free friend needs cash quickly, so he may sacrifice the price he gets, maybe letting his house go for far less than it's actually worth.

What about our other laid-off executive, also a homeowner? Remember, she took our advice on taking out a $400,000 mortgage rather than paying for the house outright. That means she still has $400,000 in cash or investments that she can access. Her job situation is tough—she still has to find work—but in the meantime, her money is generating cash flow (interest, dividends, or capital gains) toward her expenses, and she has access to the assets. She's far more likely to be able to weather this storm. But she has other options: If she goes to the bank for a home equity loan, having a comfortable cushion of investments makes it far likelier that she'll get that loan.

Finally, she will not have to sell the house quickly and sacrifice its value. Even if she eventually has to move to another city or state, she can take her time to get the highest possible value for the property.

The person who has no accessible liquid assets and no debt has few or no options. The person who has accessible liquid assets and debt has many options and is safer.

<table>
<tr><th colspan="2">Figure 4: Debt Decision #1</th></tr>
<tr><td colspan="2">Assumptions:
• Both have $500,000 of liquid investments or cash.
• Both wish to buy a house for $500,000.</td></tr>
<tr><th>Person A</th><th>Person B</th></tr>
<tr><td>1. Puts down $500,000 for house</td><td>1. Puts down $100,000 for house</td></tr>
<tr><td>2. Has no mortgage (or cash left)</td><td>2. Obtains a $400,000 mortgage and invests the $400,000 left over from the original $500,000.</td></tr>
<tr><td colspan="2">Both A and B lose their jobs in a recession.
• Who has more options?
• Who is safer?
• Who is taking advantage of compounding and the Tax Savings Savings Effect?
• Who will probably achieve their financial goals first?
• Who will work longer and harder in their life?</td></tr>
</table>

Let's examine another hypothetical, shown in figure 5, that relates to the idea of debt but that also illustrates how you can put yourself behind in your financial plan due to a lack of understanding of the principle of compounding.

You're building wealth well, but you're only about a third of the way to your financial goal, not quite at geometric compounding. You have a home that's worth $500,000. You have a $250,000 mortgage on it. Then this house across town that you've always loved and wanted to buy comes on the market for $1 million. You decide, "I have $1 million in investment accounts, and I have worked diligently for years. I'm going to buy that house!"

So you sell your $500,000 house, pay off the $250,000 mortgage, and put the remaining $250,000 you get from the sale down on the new house. Now you have a financial choice to make: 1. You can take $750,000 from your investment accounts and wind up with no mortgage; or 2. You can take out a $750,000 mortgage (three times as high as the mortgage you had on the prior house). Last assumption: You have the cash flow to afford a $750,000 mortgage.

Figure 5: Debt Decision #2
What financial option (A or B) should you take to get to geometric compounding the fastest, work less hard and fewer years, and achieve financial independence in the shortest time frame?
Option A
1. Sell current home for $500,000 and pay off mortgage of $250,000. 2. Buy a new home for $1 million and place $250,000 from the sale of the previous home on the new home. 3. Take $750,000 from investment accounts to pay for the new home. 4. Has $250,000 left in savings and no mortgage.
Option B
1. Sell current home for $500,000 and pay off mortgage of $250,000. 2. Buy new home for $1 million and place $250,000 from the sale of the previous home on the new home. 3. Take out a $750,000 mortgage and keep $1 million in your investment accounts.
Results
• With Option A, you fall further from geometric compounding. • With Option A, you do not take advantage of compounding or the Tax Savings Savings Effect. • Option A will mean working longer and harder to achieve your financial goals.

What do you think most people would do? What would you do? Because of this obsession with being out of debt as soon as possible, certainly by the time they're retired or independent, most would pay down more of the mortgage or maybe even the whole thing. However, if you remember the principle of compounding and are working your Wealth Building Formula, you know that when you take money away from your investable wealth, you have less money that's going to compound, and it will take you more time to achieve the geometric jump. If you replace that wealth through saving, you will eventually get to the powerful part of compounding, what we refer to as geometric compounding, but it will take more years of life and more years of having to go to that office and work.

Yet people make this kind of choice based on the emotional dread of debt without realizing the effects on their financial lives. It is not difficult to see how this choice affects you. It is a matter of "running the numbers"—doing the calculations to see how your decision has a future impact on you. But people just don't take the time to do this.

Companies and people have the same choices around debt as in the examples here. Some companies start on a shoestring, don't plan cash flow properly, and don't have the cash reserves, and when something happens, there's nothing to fall back on. They can have a great business and actually be profitable, but their cash flow is poor, and they go under. Other companies start off by prudently planning debt, ensuring that they will have reserves for unforeseen events. They have a better chance of making it because they planned debt and created shareholder wealth from it. It is exactly the same with individuals.

Over the years, Al has given many lectures to business and professional groups, as well as to new professionals just graduating. While college grads average $30,000 in educational debt, many have more, especially physicians and attorneys. Many of these graduates can have more than $200,000 in student loan debt, and they leave school determined to pay it off in a three- to seven-year time frame just so they can get that "monkey" off their back.

What we explain to these recent graduates is that there are financial institutions that will let them pay this debt off over twenty-five years and that it might be a better financial choice if they are out to achieve financial independence in the shortest time frame.

Let's explore why that's so.

As an example, you could pay off your $200,000 worth of loans over five years. That is about $44,000 per year (assuming a 5 percent rate of interest). If you financed $200,000 over twenty-five years instead, assuming a 5 percent interest rate depending on the government program or bank, your annual payments with interest would be a little less than $14,000 per year. That means you save $30,000 ($44,000 - $14,000 = $30,000) of cash flow per year by extending the loans.

If you're one of these young physicians who joined a practice with a 401(k) or a pension plan, you could shelter that entire amount from income tax. Using the Tax Savings Savings Effect, this means that the total amount you could save (assuming a 40 percent combined federal and state income tax rate) could be up to $50,000 (Tax Savings Savings Effect-40 percent tax rate x $50,000 = $20,000 and $30,000 + $20,000 = $50,000).

Saving $50,000 per year, tax deferred and assuming a growth rate of 6 percent, equals a bit more than $2.9 million over those twenty-five years. Did you have to work any harder for this $2.9 million? No. Was your original student loan now paid off? Yes. For some, this choice could possibly fund their retirement wealth goals.

Maybe you only have $20,000 in debt, not $200,000, 10 percent of $200,000 or the difference of adding a zero. This does not change the financial advantage except for the total saved. You could earn $290,000 or 10 percent of the $2.9 million, have your loan paid off, without working a day longer.

Some might argue that getting the loans out of the way first and then saving the $44,000 difference per year might be better. Tell me, when you last paid off a credit card balance or a car loan, did you subsequently save the monthly amount of that payment? People don't tend to do this. Look back at our "power of compounding" illustration in tables 1 and 2, and ask yourself which it is better to be: the Go-Getter or the Slowpoke?

Make Debt Work For You, Rather Than Against You

Whether it's paying off your student loans, mortgages, or the debts in your business, the choices you make are going to affect your Wealth Building Formula. This, in turn, will affect how long you have to work, how much wealth you have when you decide to retire, and how much risk you must have in your investment portfolio.

We had a client in her late twenties who had $40,000 in loans and owned a house with $100,000 in equity. She said that she wanted to start saving but could not. She wanted to pay off her loans over the next five years, and then she'd save.

"You have a house and you have some equity in it," we told her. "Your loans are $40,000. Why don't you just take out a home equity loan and pay off the loans now so that you can start saving those monthly payments right now into your 401(k) at work?"

How would this work to her advantage? She was paying about $1,700 a month for the loans. Immediately, she could start to save a lot more because a home equity payment cost (assuming a rate of 10 percent) only $333 per month (10 percent x $40k = $4k, $4k/12 = $333/month). She could now save $1,367 ($1,700 - $333 = $1,367) per month or $16,404 per year (12 X $1,367= $16,404). She would have contributions to place in her 401(k) and get tax benefits (via the Tax Savings Savings Effect) for an additional $10,936 or a total of savings of $27,340 (40 percent x $27,340 = $10,936, $16,404 + $10,936= $27,340) and could contribute a total of $27,340 per year to her 401(k) or tax-deferred plan.

If she saved $27,340 per year over thirty years, assuming a growth rate of 6 percent, she could have a total of almost $2.3 million, all by simply "shuffling paper," or filling out and processing paperwork for the loans, not by working an hour longer. This loan payment strategy was a multimillion-dollar decision that worked powerfully in her favor. It should be noted that if you are going to use debt smarter, you must save the difference to get the real benefit. If you are not, then you might as well pay down the debt.

When you're looking at debt as a way to create wealth, remember: Saving now rather than later means that you'll take advantage of the principle of compounding. If you really do want to pay off your debt eventually, pay it off when you don't need to save anymore or at the end of your plan. Most people pay their debt down quickly at the beginning, which sentences them to work longer and harder. If you believe in the principle of compounding and the Tax Savings Savings Effect, that is how—and when—you pay off debt.

As we've noted, many people do it the exact opposite way—pay debt off quicker. They'll put an extra month's payment on their mortgage every year. They'll pay an extra few hundreds or thousands of dollars a month to get that debt down. That goes against the principle of compounding and the Tax Savings Savings Effect—it makes your taxes higher and you end up having to work longer and harder. So why would you?

Don't Be Caught In Depression-Era Ideas

Make your relationship with debt a healthy one, with you in the driver's seat. Don't let your attitudes toward it be dictated by emotions, what you've been told in the past, or a Depression-era mindset.

Most people don't use debt smarter because they don't have a way to make better financial decisions. If you know your Wealth Building

Formula and understand the power of compounding and of the Tax Savings Savings Effect, you have the option of using debt smarter to get to your goals faster, have more wealth when you get there, or reduce the risk in your investment portfolio, without having to work one day longer in life.

— Application Box —
Amin's Debt Upgrade, Not "Debt Panic" (Manage It Like A Refinance)

A lot of advice says, "Pay it off as fast as possible." Here is a smarter way to think about it: Debt is a tool. The goal is to protect cash flow and upgrade bad debt into better debt, not spiral into shame.

So don't manage debt emotionally. Do yourself a favor, just run the numbers and make the best monthly cash flow choice.

Use the three-number check:

- APR (what it costs)
- fees (what it takes to move)
- flexibility (what happens if life gets messy)

Debt Upgrade Flow

- Step one: List every debt (balance, APR, minimum payment, due date).
- Step two: Label it.
    - Bad debt: high APR and revolving/with heavy fees (credit cards, payday, many buy now, pay later/store cards)
    - Better debt: lower APR, longer term, fixed payoff, predictable payment
- Step three: Choose one upgrade path.
    - Credit union consolidation loan (often a strong first stop)

    - 0 percent balance transfer card (if your credit is strong enough)
    - Refinance/restructure with current lender (hardship plan, APR reduction)
    - Student loan—use caution (don't trade protections away blindly)
- Step four: Run a break-even check (the interest and fees are the same or less than what you have to pay before).
    - When this happens, the break-even is reasonable, the upgrade is worth it.
- Step five: Execute one move and automate payments.

Why Start With A Credit Union?

Credit unions are member-owned and often price loans more favorably. Bankrate cites an average rate of approximately 10.72 percent for a three-year personal loan at credit unions (NCUA data, Q3 2025).[32]

Also, federal credit unions have a temporary 18 percent interest rate ceiling extended into 2027.[33]

And here's the practical reality: The average credit card APR was approximately 20.97 percent in Q4 2025.[34]

So even a "not perfect" consolidation APR can still be a meaningful upgrade if it slows or stops the bleed.

How To Know If A Personal Loan Rate Is "Good"

Use this simple lens:

- If you're currently at around 21 percent on credit cards, anything materially lower can be an upgrade.
- Credit union personal loans around 10–12 percent are often competitive benchmarks.

- If you're quoted near the 18 percent ceiling, it may still help versus cards—but you should also explore other paths (APR reduction call, balance transfer, cosigner, credit-builder options).

Hidden-Fee Checklist (Ask This Before You Sign)

APR is supposed to reflect the cost of credit, including certain fees—not just the interest rate.

Still, you need to verify details. Ask for the Truth-in-Lending disclosure and ask these questions:

- Is there an origination fee? (How much? Is it deducted from the loan?)
- Is there any prepayment penalty? (Can I pay early for free?)
- What is the late fee amount and grace period?
- Is the rate fixed or variable?
- Are there any required or automatic add-ons? (insurance, memberships—are they optional or required?)
- Are there any payment method fees? (pay by card fee, expedited payment fee)

Red flag: any lender asking for an upfront fee before giving you the loan—the FTC explicitly warns that's a common scam.

Bank Versus Credit Union: Which Should You Call?

If your goal is upgrading expensive debt while protecting cash flow:

- Start with credit unions (often lower rates/more flexible underwriting).
- Then compare one bank and one reputable online lender, so you have real options.

If You're In College: Is There A University Credit Union?

Often, yes—many credit unions have membership rules tied to a community, employer, or school "field of membership."

Practical move: Search "[Your university] credit union" or check your school's student resources page. Even if there's no "official" one, you may qualify through where you live or work.

What If Your Credit Score Isn't High?

You still have upgrade options—just different ones:

- Ask a credit union about a smaller consolidation loan (or a credit-builder loan) to improve terms over time.
- Use a cosigner only if you have a clear payoff plan and automation in place.
- If you can't refinance yet: Call your current card issuer and ask for an APR reduction or hardship program while you rebuild.

Your One Move This Week

- Call one local credit union and ask for a consolidation quote.
- Compare it using the three-number check (APR/fees/flexibility).
- If it's an upgrade, execute the move and automate the payment.

That's not debt panic. That's a debt upgrade, and it protects your cash flow so your Wealth Building Formula can actually work.

CakeClub Slices

- Debt can be a tool to build wealth.
- Convert bad (higher interest, shorter term) debt to good debt (lower interest rate, longer term) but save the difference.
- People with debt and savings are safer (from sudden events) than those with no debt and no savings.
- Perform "debt upgrades" when you can. Save the difference.
- Consider workout specialists (attorneys, others) when negotiating with credit card companies and banks if you find it difficult to do yourself.

9

Other Ways To Find Investable Cash

I have enough money to last the rest of my life . . .
unless I buy something.
—Jackie Mason, comedian and actor

Are you guilty of "financial flexing" to impress others?

We've already seen how finding more investable cash can move you toward your goals more quickly. But how and where can you most easily find it?

One of the first places you should look is at your own spending. Our philosophy around personal financial planning and spending is that you should live life the way you wish and not have to scrape to preserve, manage, or add to your wealth to get to your financial goals. But there are some meaningful ways to cut your spending without sacrificing your quality of life—in fact, some you might not feel it at all.

A 2025 nationwide study from Credit One Bank found that more than half of Gen Z admit to lying or exaggerating about their financial success online. According to a December 3, 2025, article in *USA TODAY*, "Gen Z is 'financial flexing.' Why they're going broke to look successful." The article raises serious points about spending:

> Aja Evans, a licensed mental health counselor and financial therapist, says that Gen Z also wants to show the best of the best of what their life might look like, even though many of these luxuries aren't realistic on an everyday American salary, especially for young people starting in the workforce.
>
> "People will push themselves past their own financial boundaries to spend more to make sure that they're looking a certain way online because it appears as if everybody is looking that same way," Evans says.
>
> Those habits extend to people's dating lives, too. The study found that 38 percent of people admit to going into debt or damaging their credit score to impress someone, and those rates are higher among men, 46 percent of whom said they'd overdraft their accounts to impress their date.
>
> Evans says she sees "financial flexing" in some of her clients, though they might not recognize it that way. It can come up with weddings and bachelor trips, destination birthdays, and engagement parties, when a client considers going into debt because they don't want to miss out or seem like an uninvolved friend.[35]

Discipline By Design

Most people treat self-control like a personality trait. It's not. It's an environmental problem. In food research, small changes in visibility, convenience, simple labeling, and smarter placement shift what people choose, even when the menu stays the same. One well-known cafeteria study found that adding clear "traffic light" labels and making healthier items easier to grab increased healthier purchases (without banning anything).[36]

Money works the same way. Your environment is already engineered, just not for you. It's engineered for frictionless checkout, saved cards, autorenew, and "sure, why not?" spending. And when paying feels more frictionless, people tend to spend more. A large 2024 meta-analysis (392 effect sizes from seventy-one papers) found a small but significant "cashless effect," meaning spending is higher with cashless payments than with cash.[37]

So, you don't eliminate temptation. You redesign the environment so that the better decision becomes the default.

— Application Box —

Amin's Three Money Levers (Simple, Powerful, Unfairly Effective)

Make the truth obvious (visibility wins).

If you can't see it, you can't manage it. Money "disappears" when it's fragmented, on different cards, different accounts, different apps. The fix is a single view that turns spending into something you can recognize. Tools like the CakeClub app help by letting you connect accounts/cards (or add transactions manually), categorize spending, and set a spending plan so patterns stop hiding in plain sight.

Make expensive choices slightly annoying (friction saves money).

You don't need a ban. You need a pause, just enough to interrupt autopilot.

- Remove the most tempting apps.
- Turn off one-click checkout.
- Require Face ID for purchases.

- Move shopping apps off your home screen (yes, this is the adult version of putting cookies on the top shelf).

Put the good choice on autopilot (defaults do the heavy lifting).
Don't rely on "I'll be good this month." Build a system that works when you're tired, stressed, or hungry. A default can be tiny: an alert, a weekly check-in, a rule that new subscriptions require a twenty-four-hour wait. The goal is simple: fewer "in-the-moment" decisions, more "already-decided" wins. If you don't know how, ask CakeClub AI chat agent.

One rule to remember:

If a goal matters, don't store it in your motivation. Store it in your environment.

It Happens When You're Not Looking

The fact is that people get very busy and consequently do things that waste cash flow that would otherwise be there for their lifestyle or for adding to their wealth.

A good starting point for reclaiming this waste is to look at arrangements that you might have, such as subscriptions for streaming services or apps, and memberships. We had a client who used LegalZoom and another app to create a simple will. She did not realize they were charging her a monthly fee for months after she stopped using them. You might have monthly fees of $200 or more, which results in $2,400 per year.

Many of our clients have to evaluate whether they are using their gym membership. They have it charged to their credit cards, and they don't keep track of it. If you are, don't end it, but if you are not using it or you can do your workout at home, great.

Even small things can add up when you take the power of compounding and the Tax Savings Savings Effect into consideration. Remember, these expenses are not tax-deductible, so saving $3,000 per year and saving it in your 401(k) or IRA (if deductible) can cause total savings to be $5,000. A lot of people, personally or in business, will subscribe to online news outlets or magazines, spending hundreds of dollars a month but never really looking at them. This may seem small, but with the power of compounding, it could be a multimillion-dollar decision over time.

People will use their credit cards and not pay them off in a timely fashion. This can cost thousands of dollars over time in penalties and extra interest. They have the cash flow, yet they incur a lot of unnecessary and avoidable charges by ignoring the payment due dates. There are specialty cards that charge you up to $400 or $500 a year to be a cardholder. Do you really need that added card and expense? Maybe not. Yes, these are relatively small amounts, but remember compounding and the Tax Savings Savings Effect.

— Application Box —
Amin's Subscription Board Meeting: Run Your Life Like A CFO

Subscriptions are the silent line items in modern cash flow. They are frictionless, automatic, and invisible, which is exactly why they grow without permission.

And the data is clear: People consistently underestimate what they spend on them.

Recent research shows that American Gen Z consumers spend an average of $377 per month on subscriptions, depending on how broadly these services are defined.[38] That totals $4,524 per year leaving their accounts quietly and automatically.

Meanwhile, more than half of Americans (about 55 percent) admit they have at least one unused subscription, wasting around $10–$11 per month on services they don't use.[39]

Streaming alone illustrates the pattern:

- The average U.S. household now pays for about four to six streaming services. [40]
- They are spending roughly $60–$109 per month on them.[41]
- And 34 percent of subscribers say they cut other household spending just to keep subscriptions active.[42, 43]

This is a cash-flow awareness problem. Subscriptions are the personal-finance version of software licenses inside a company. No CFO lets software autorenew forever without review. Your life deserves the same discipline.

The Subscription Board Meeting (Twenty-Minute Exercise)

Think of this as your quarterly personal finance board meeting. Open the CakeClub app (or app you are using) and find your recurring transactions and see all your subscriptions.

- Step one: List every subscription.
    - Streaming, apps, software, memberships, delivery perks, newsletters, cloud storage, fitness, gaming, AI tools, everything.
- Step two: Convert monthly cost to annual cost.
    - Multiply by twelve.
    - A $9.99 subscription is not $10. It's $120 per year. Five small subscriptions can easily become $600–$1,200 per year without you noticing. That's real cash flow.

- Step three: Classify each subscription.
    - Label each one:
        - weekly value
        - monthly value
        - rarely used
        - Be honest, not optimistic.
- Step four: Cancel one "rarely used" subscription today.
    - Not tomorrow. Not later. Today. Immediate action reduces friction and increases follow-through, especially when a decision is already made.
- Step five: Move the freed money to your savings account.
    - Immediately. Not "later." Not "when you remember." Immediately.

Why This Works

Subscriptions exploit three psychological tendencies:

- Automation blindness. Automatic payments reduce the "pain of paying," making spending less noticeable.
- Small-payment illusion. A $7.99 decision feels trivial, but repeated monthly, it becomes meaningful.
- Identity inertia. People keep subscriptions because they once imagined becoming "the person who uses them."

The subscription board meeting breaks all three.

You restore:

- awareness
- intention
- control

The Real Goal

This is not about becoming anti-subscription. Subscriptions can be fantastic tools.

Some can deliver enormous value:

- learning platforms
- fitness memberships you actually use
- productivity tools
- community memberships
- entertainment you love

The rule is simple: If it earns its keep, keep it. If it doesn't, redirect the cash flow. That is not budgeting. That is capital allocation. That is how a CFO thinks. And that is how financial independence actually begins: not with deprivation, but with intentional cash-flow design.

Check Your Rates

A simple way to keep track of your cash flow and where it's going is to make sure that every once in a while, you and your financial expert are looking at your credit card interest rates and balances. Maybe having your credit cards' balances refinanced into a personal line of credit or your home equity would save you money. Can you do better?

Even if you have a business, having business loans refinanced can sometimes save thousands, if not tens of thousands of dollars. We recently saved a business more than $10,000 a year in investable cash by negotiating rates and payouts.

A client was in the office just recently; we had asked her a few times to provide us with information about her mortgage, but she'd gotten busy and hadn't done so. When she finally got around to it, we discovered that she was paying about 8 percent, much more than she should have been. Refinancing saved her thousands a year.

Other Ways To Find Cash Flow

What are some other places where you might find more investable cash? As we discussed earlier, we encourage employees to review their company benefits programs to make certain they're taking full advantage of them, like being sure to fill up their 401(k)—since most companies match. Is there a deferred bonus system? A deferred compensation plan at work could potentially help you to save thousands of dollars a year. Are there stock options plans that you're not invested in?

Are there free or low-cost life and disability insurance programs? When it comes to life insurance, sometimes an employer plan allows you to pay less through group coverage than if you were to buy life insurance outside of the group. The same benefit can extend to either disability insurance or long-term care.

Sometimes employers don't offer these benefits, and of course if you change employers, you may lose some of these, but you may find that going to another employer will garner the same or greater benefits.

What we're talking about here is again what we call "shuffling paper," filling out forms and not working one hour longer or any harder. It's just a matter of looking at the day-to-day financial choices you are making and choosing to make better ones.

What are some other ways to find investable cash? When you're dealing with your current employer, discuss what your future holds. What does your position look like in two, five, or ten years? Is there any way to improve your skills? What's the opportunity for growth, not only in terms of promotion or position but in your compensation and any other benefits that you could get?

Is it possible to structure your compensation in some other way? We have had some employees structure new positions for themselves as independent contractors or consultants. They actually made more money—30 to 40 percent more cash flow in some cases—because the employer did not have to pay for all the benefits they'd had to before.

Is there a side gig opportunity like Uber, DoorDash, or using computer skills to help businesses build websites? Maybe become a part-time personal assistant, a real estate agent? Many find extra cash flow working part-time while holding their full-time positions.

As a self-employed contractor, you might be eligible to start your own pension plan and have access to myriad other ways to shelter your income that you could not as an employee. You might qualify for a home office tax deduction, along with other business expense deductions that you couldn't take before, leading you to more investable cash.

If you've been a successful employee, but maybe unappreciated by your employer, you may want to investigate how valuable you could be to someone else. It doesn't have to be a competitor; it can be an employer that has a need for someone in the same position as yours, perhaps in a different industry.

Finding Cash Flow In Your Business

What if you're a business owner? What are some ways to find investable cash there? Even though some firms offer a 401(k) plan, they may not fully fund it. Sometimes there's the misperception that you can't have a 401(k) plan and also fund an IRA, which is not true. Especially for small businesses, see if you can have what's called a *defined benefit plan* or, more commonly today, a cash balance plan.

We worked with two business owners in the Midwest; their firm had about ten employees. The owners both made good money in their company, but they only had 401(k)s. With our help, they put together a cash balance pension plan and eventually were able to save another $20,000 each ($40,000) in their pension plan, which in their tax bracket (between federal and state it was almost 50 percent) saved almost $20,000

(50 percent x $40,000 = $20,000) in income taxes. These tax savings paid for half of the $40,000 they put away in the pension plan. So the government helped them fund their pensions. This is not unusual.

As a business owner, when was the last time you took a serious look at your operating costs? How effective are your billing department and your accounts receivable policies? Sometimes you get sloppy in those areas, so you don't collect in a timely fashion. That carelessness can cost you tens of thousands of dollars in cash flow.

Are you charging enough for your services? We worked with a popular and successful young life coach who was working all kinds of hours. But he didn't seem to be able to get ahead in terms of living the lifestyle he wanted to, paying his taxes, and putting aside what he had to save to eventually achieve his financial goals within the time frame he wanted.

We sat down with him and said, "Why don't you double your prices? Instead of charging $2,500 a day, why not charge $5,000 a day?"

Of course, at first, he was shocked by this idea. What would his clients think?

We said, "Well, why don't you test it? Test it on a new client, since you're already very busy."

He did that, and to his surprise, he found out that it had very little impact. Just by charging more for his time, he was able to dramatically increase his income without raising his expenses or working longer hours. Again, he was "shuffling paper," not working harder.

Small businesses need to have clear earnings targets. Imagine if Apple's Tim Cook announced that he had no idea what their earnings would be in an upcoming quarter; their stockholders would not be pleased. Another thing we find often with small businesses is that they don't have budgets. We think this is a critical thing for a firm.

Another mistake businesses often make is failing to check their benefits packages for their employees often enough. If you're the owner of a small business and you offer health insurance, long-term care, life insurance, or any other type of benefit, it's important to have your packages reviewed at least once each year. We do this on a regular basis with our business clients. We can think of more than a few examples where clients have saved tens of thousands of dollars (depending on the size of their operations).

Remember, saving "only" hundreds per month can add up to tens of thousands over time. Not only that, sometimes they're even able to enhance the benefits they provide. We're not suggesting that employers decrease their employees' benefits; by realizing that products and offerings change, you can save tremendous amounts of money by simply "shuffling paper."

Are You Overpaying For Insurance?

People are very familiar with insurance, whether it's life insurance, long-term care, disability, or property and casualty insurance that covers your home, auto, and listed personal property (like jewelry and art).

But what is insurance, really? In life, we decide that there are risks that we are willing to be responsible for ourselves, but there are others that we're not willing to gamble on.

For instance, you might decide that you're not going to get long-term care insurance, because your family has good genes and tends to live long and healthy lives. Thus, you're willing to assume the (hopefully small) risk that the same won't also be true for you. But you're not willing to assume the risk of replacing your house if it burns down or if a client slips and falls in your hallway. In buying insurance, we're effectively hiring a third party to assume that risk: the at-fault insurance company.

As your wealth increases, you may someday accrue assets such as art, jewelry, wine, and cars. All of these things might need to be insured. You also need to be insured on your home or rental property. All of your property insurance coverage needs to be reviewed, especially if you're in multiple states, to see that you're protected properly, to potentially enhance your protection, and to be sure that you're not paying more than you need to.

One of our clients was a young entrepreneur who owned a couple of rental properties and had multiple insurance policies. He had one property in the Massachusetts area that had damage one year, and he filed a claim. He didn't realize that the insurance company raised the insurance rate on that property from $1,200 a year to $4,000 a year because of that claim. His partner handles all of the property bills, and he didn't pay attention to this kind of thing.

But it was our job. We found a new insurance company that came in and enhanced the coverage of that property while also returning the rate to about $1,200 a year. We saved him and his partner $2,800 a year just by looking at what they were paying.

When was the last time that you heard from your property and casualty insurance agent? We're betting never. When was the last time that you had your coverage reviewed? If you haven't heard from your agent or haven't reviewed your coverage and costs in the last year or two, you should have this done.

One coverage area that is normally the least costly type of insurance but people don't keep up with it or even don't have at all is personal liability insurance. This is a type of insurance you may want to explore if you have built some savings or have a home or a rental property.

Personal liability insurance protects you from your negligent acts worldwide. If someone falls down a flight of steps in your home, is injured, and sues you, personal liability insurance covers that. If you're in a shopping mall halfway around the world and you accidentally bump someone who falls down the escalator and they sue you because they receive serious injuries, you are protected by having this insurance.

You probably already have some personal liability coverage insurance built into your home and auto policies, but you may want to add additional personal liability insurance because those other policies sometimes only cover you for half a million or a million dollars. Even though these are events you're unlikely to experience, you could be sued for millions of dollars for a simple accident. You want to make sure that you're covered for that—the good news here is that these policies are very, very inexpensive.

We once advised a client who had his own consulting business and did not have this coverage to get it, and he did, after some procrastination. Not two months later, he was involved in a tragic car accident in which he hit a car that had suddenly stopped ahead of him. He was only going fifteen miles per hour. It would have been a minor fender bender, except that the passenger in the car he hit was a very frail, elderly woman. The jolt snapped her head back, and she had to be rushed to the hospital, where she spent three or four months before she passed away—all because of that simple accident. It was a very unusual, catastrophic event.

When he was served with the resulting million-dollar lawsuit from the family and hospital, he called us up in a panic and said, "What do I do?"

We told him, "Call the insurance company, and they will handle everything for you. You are protected totally from the damage and attorneys' fees." Ever since, he's been our poster child for making sure our clients have personal liability insurance. He's the only one of our clients who has ever had to use it, but it preserved his wealth.

Nobody enjoys contemplating worst-case scenarios, but even so, another important piece of your contingency planning should be life insurance. If you are single and have no partner, you may not need this. If so, don't waste money here.

However, life insurance is initially bought to fill gaps in your wealth. If it's important to you to leave behind enough wealth for your loved ones to live the life you wish for them in the event of your death, you get this coverage. When that gap doesn't exist anymore, you might decide that you no longer need life insurance.

But before making that choice and as part of your financial plan, you should explore what life insurance can do as another asset class that allows your money and wealth to grow tax-free. As you build wealth over the years, it can also be instrumental in your estate planning, including helping your heirs to avoid paying estate taxes or in creating a legacy for your family, such as for a college or charity.

Perhaps you wish to leave a scholarship to a college or an endowment to an art museum someday in the future. Or you want to fund a trust for your grandchildren and great-grandchildren to make sure they're all educated. Life insurance can be used for any of those purposes, and the process is not complex.

Though this may be far in the future for you, we've even shown clients how life insurance can be used to create a secure, future, tax-free stream of income that we have referred to sometimes as a "proxy pension plan." This can be a great way to create more investable cash, tax-free.

Finally, review your healthcare, long-term disability, and long-term care coverages. While these policies can protect your wealth, you might find some opportunities to save investable cash.

Put On Your Oxygen Mask First

If you are married with kids, read the following. If not, skip this for now and just concentrate on saving for yourself.

One common use for investable cash is a very personal choice: the education of your children. Most look at setting up a 529 plan or an account under the Uniform Gifts to Minors Act (UGMA) for their children to save for education. If you're in this group, you may want to consider what we call the "airline rule" first.

On a flight, you are told that in the event the oxygen masks drop down, you should put yours on first before assisting your child. If you can take care of yourself first, then both you and the child will be OK. We feel the same way when it comes to putting aside wealth for education. If you take care of yourself first, they will be fine. We think that's especially true when it comes to a UGMA. At first, you start to put wealth away in the account, and you are the trustee. Because of the cost of college, these accounts can get into the hundreds of thousands of dollars.

But what happens when your child turns eighteen? When they attain their "majority" age, they're now empowered to run their own affairs. That means that if you've poured money into a UGMA for a child's education, when they turn eighteen, they can decide to use that wealth any way they wish—maybe to "ponder life" for a few years on the beaches of Malibu.

If you put the money into a 529 plan, you have more control, but the rate of return is poor on most of these accounts, and fees can be high. If instead you accumulate wealth and add more wealth to what you have, you're going to control how it's spent, hit geometric compounding sooner, achieve your financial plan sooner, and be able to take care of your children.

Not everyone agrees with this philosophically, and that's OK. You make the decisions. Just remember that we're out to make sure you're taken care of first.

You can see that there are myriad ways in which you can find new cash flow without adding to your work hours or years of work life or suffering any lifestyle deprivation, simply by making better and smarter choices in different areas of your financial life.

We've just covered a few here; there are many, many more. Be creative. Taking the time to sit down with a good personal financial planner who will give you a structure to look at all these variables annually is probably well worth the time, effort, and money. A good wealth adviser will help you with this—and with the creation of an overall financial plan based on your long-term investment return objective, which we'll discuss in the next chapter.

— Application Box —
Amin's Seven-Day Leak Freeze: Turn "Making Visible" Into A Cash-Flow Game

Ask someone to "save more" and you'll often hear, "Save on what?" That answer is honest. Most spending isn't one big decision; it's a set of small defaults you've repeated so often they disappear from view.

And when money is tight, it gets worse. Financial pressure consumes mental bandwidth and can measurably reduce cognitive performance.

So here's a better approach: Don't punish yourself. Run experiments. Find cash flow. Then choose what stays.

Why This Game Works

- It makes the invisible visible. People consistently underestimate recurring spending. As we mentioned previously, in one survey, consumers guessed they spent $86 per month on subscriptions; itemizing showed $219 per month on average (about 2.5 times higher).[44]
- It replaces willpower with a script. "If, then" plans (implementation intentions) have a medium-to-large positive effect on follow-through across many studies.[45] In other words, it removes decision-making in the moment. You write one rule before temptation shows up: "If *X* happens, I do *Y*." That way, you don't negotiate with yourself under pressure.
- It turns "no" into a reward you can see. Research on earmarking/partitioning shows people save more when money is labeled and separated instead of pooled.[46] It makes progress visible and makes it harder to steal from

yourself. When you move the "would-have-spent" money into a separate, clearly labeled bucket the same day, your brain treats it as already assigned—so you're less likely to casually spend it later.

An Exercise

Pick one leak for your first round.

Choose one category, just one:

- delivery apps
- coffee runs
- convenience store snacks
- one "optional" subscription tier
- impulse online shopping
- rideshare instead of transit/carpool

The Rules (Simple, Specific, Temporary)

Run a seven-day freeze on that category only.

Not forever. Not everything. Just that one leak.

Examples:

- "No delivery this week. Groceries or pickup only."
- "No paid coffee. Home coffee only."
- "Downgrade Netflix subscription tier for one month."

The Seven-Day Leak Freeze Playbook

- Step one: Choose the freeze.
    - Write: "For the next seven days, I'm freezing: ____."
- Step two: Predecide your weak moment (if, then).
    - Pick the moment you usually break and script it:
- "If I want delivery, then I eat what I already have, and pickup is allowed tomorrow."

- "If I want coffee out, then I make coffee at home and move the saved amount into my bucket."
- Step three: The most important move: transfer the "would-have-spent" money the same day.
    - Create a separate bucket (separate account or labeled savings sub-bucket).
    - Every time you skip the purchase, immediately move the amount you would have spent.
    - This is the magic. You're not just saying "no." You're converting a habit into visible progress.
- Step four: Keep score like a game.
    - Track three numbers:
- wins: how many times you avoided the leak
- loot: total dollars moved into the bucket
- replacement: what you did instead (groceries, pickup, home coffee, walk, etc.)
- Step five: End the week with one decision.
    - Don't ask, "Can I do this forever?"
    - Ask, "What's worth keeping now that I can see the real cost?"
    - Then choose:
- keep it (but with a limit)
- downgrade it
- cut it and redirect that cash flow

A Quick Example (So You Can Feel It)

You freeze delivery for seven days. You normally order three times per week at $25 all-in.

That could be $75 you just found, without changing who you are or "living like a monk." Of course you still have to eat, but maybe you make something less expensive at home. Let's say you save $50.

Now you choose on purpose:

- Put $25 into your Freedom Floor (your automatic minimum that moves you forward whenever money hits).
- Keep $25 as fun money, because the point is a life you enjoy now and feel safer later.

Try It This Week

Pick one leak. Freeze it for seven days.

Transfer the "would-have-spent" money the same day into a separate bucket.

Then decide what stays in your life, on purpose.

That isn't budgeting. That's reclaiming cash flow and upgrading your defaults.

CakeClub Slices

- Cash flow is wasted when you don't see it. Make sure all spending is visible.
- Have a "subscription board meeting" and run your finances like a CFO.
- Review annual contracts like health, life, personal liability, and warranties and shop for better cost proposals.
- Save for yourself first, others later.
- Play the seven-day leak freeze and turn "making visible" into a cash-flow game.

10

What Being A Savvy Investor Really Means

Knowing Your Long-Term Investment Return Objective

Investing should be more like watching paint dry or watching grass grow. If you want excitement, take $800 and go to Las Vegas.
—Paul Samuelson, economist

Why is having a good investment plan so important? The obvious reason is that people want to have a healthy and safe return on their money. How do most people invest?

According to a January 2026 report by the World Economic Forum, Gen Z invests very differently from previous generations. The report raises interesting points:

About a third started investing in university or early adulthood, which is double the rate of Millennials investing at that age. Moreover,

> more than 50% of Gen Z individuals surveyed by the Forum said they started to learn about investing before entering the workforce, compared to only about 20% of baby boomers.
>
> Many factors contribute to this. Firstly, Gen Z is navigating a world where they must shoulder more of the risk for their personal, long-term financial stability instead of relying on government social safety nets or workplace pensions. In addition, the ubiquity of smartphones and the proliferation of financial applications have made investing easily accessible around the clock.[47]

People love to talk about their investments when they really hit a home run, which is why at house parties or casual hangouts, you're likely to hear something like, "I invested in Apple stock many years ago. I've earned 300 percent or 400 percent." You never hear people talk about when they invested in something that didn't turn out as well.

But whether they've done well or not is not the real issue. The one thing you might want to ask them is, "What is your long-term investment return objective?"

Whenever we ask that, we find that most just stare at us blankly. "What do you mean?"

Sometimes they'll offer some general answers, but when we press the question—what percent return do they "need" to achieve their short-term and long-term savings and cash-flow goals?—they cannot tell us.

When Apple executives invest in developing a product, they're looking for a return on equity for their shareholders, and they have multiple products to choose from to develop. But whatever they choose, there's a long-term investment return objective they are aiming for to make the overall return they feel they need to keep and attract new shareholders.

As a well-run company, Merck had a "portfolio" of choices when it was looking at producing a new drug. Their portfolio was an array of drugs they could choose to produce. When Al worked at Merck, he remembers once touring a factory where the production of a drug was to start. All of a sudden, the production was halted. That factory was gutted, and its equipment was replaced with tens of millions of dollars of new equipment to produce something else. Al remembers thinking to himself, "Wow, what a waste."

It wasn't until Al thought about it more deeply that he realized that it wasn't a waste of their money; they'd made a choice to make another investment that they believed would be far more profitable in their product portfolio, that would have the greatest probability of achieving their long-term investment rate objective or the rate of return they were targeting of their own Wealth Building Formula.

It's the same process when you are looking at the percent return of your Wealth Building Formula and the investment choices in your investment portfolio. Most investors just look at beating the S&P 500, the Dow, or some other index over a given time period. If they beat them in the latest quarter, they're happy. If they didn't, they're unhappy—but that is not a long-term investment return objective. A long-term investment return objective is about the rate of return, on average, over a long time period with ups and downs in the market—that's going to make your plan work and the probability that your wealth and eventual cash flow needs are achievable at the least possible risk.

Our Investment Philosophy, Approach, And Methodology

If you are going to be looking for or using an investment adviser, you want to be dealing with an adviser who has a sound philosophy, approach, and methodology to investing your hard-earned money. According to our philosophy, you should:

- Set a reasonably attainable investment return objective.
- Let compounding play a key role in growing your wealth. Let the investment cash remain in place for a long time to allow the

power of compounding to become a significant contributor to your wealth accumulation.

- Invest for the long term. A lot of people say they're long-term investors, but when the market dips in a correction or has a crash, you see them making knee-jerk reactions. Investing for the long term means not changing course because of short-term fluctuations in the market. Don't chase investment fads.
- Don't try to be a market timer. Nobody has succeeded second-guessing timing around market fluctuations in the long term.
- Only make investments that allow you to sleep well at night. Make sure you know what your adviser is doing, and be well-informed about those choices.

Base your portfolio asset allocation decisions and investment selections on what you need in the Wealth Building Formula of your personal financial plan to either accumulate the wealth you want or add to it, and to do so at the least possible risk.

Your personal philosophy may be different; your adviser's may, too, but at least make sure they have one, that you understand it, and that it gives you confidence.

What's Your Adviser's Approach?

What kind of approach do they take to investing? How do they set about actually investing?

Our approach follows the modern portfolio theory (MPT). MPT was created by Harry Markowitz, a Nobel Prize-winning economist, in his paper "Portfolio Selection."[48] It is an investment theory based on the idea that risk-averse investors can create investment portfolios to optimize or maximize expected return based on a given level of market risk. It is one of the most important and influential economic theories of its time, dealing with finance and investment.[49]

MPT essentially says that it is possible to construct an optimal investment portfolio that offers the best possible expected return for a given level of risk. By investing across asset classes such as stocks and bonds, you can benefit from diversification, which reduces portfolio risk. You reduce risk by not putting all of your eggs in one investment "basket."

What Is Your Adviser's Methodology?

What procedures or processes do they have for money manager selection?

For example, when we select money or fund managers, we look for those who deliver strong long-term performance, have a below-average risk profile for their investment style, and stay consistent in their approach. We have processes and procedures in place to accomplish this.

This isn't meant to be an investment selection book; one could write volumes on that topic alone. That said, we do wish to offer you a process by which to select an investment adviser.

The most important considerations in selecting an investment adviser are their philosophy, approach, and methodology. Your financial planner should first determine your Wealth Building Formula, which will tell you the long-term investment return objective required from your investment portfolio to achieve your wealth-building, wealth-preservation, and cash-flow requirements.

Risk And Return

Are you comfortable with and willing to accept certain degrees of investment risk required to seek to achieve the investment rate of return you need? If you're not, then lower the rate of return until you are.

Discuss this with your investment adviser and/or wealth adviser (which can be the same person, assuming they are properly qualified). If you have a Wealth Building Formula, you know that if you increase the percent return, then the other variables like *T* (time) and *C* (investable cash needed) will decrease. You will achieve what you wish in less time and with less wealth. Or, on the right side of the equation, you will have more $$$ (wealth and cash flow).

Knowing your risk tolerance (how you feel about possible decreases in value of your portfolio) is important to sleeping well at night.

In earlier chapters we've written about how finding investable cash can reduce the risk necessary in your portfolio. As a simple example, suppose that you have a $100,000 investment portfolio and you determine by your Wealth Building Formula that your percent return or your long-term investment return objective should be 6 percent. However, suppose you find a way to generate and save additional investable money through our Integrated Cash Flow Management process. Since you have found and saved this additional cash flow, you may be able to reduce your percent return to less than 6 percent, thus lowering the risk in your investment portfolio.

If you want more cash flow from your wealth, and you cannot find more investable cash elsewhere, then the return you receive from your portfolio has to increase, which will increase your risk.

By determining the cash flow required in your financial plan, you're going to determine what the return target is that you need to hit for your portfolio. Then you can make an informed investment decision based on that and how you wish to invest your money.

The higher the rate of return you choose, the greater the risk you assume. The lower the rate of return you choose, the less risk is involved. If you are a person who does not like a lot of risk, then you might choose a lower rate of return. Finding more investable cash and opportunities will allow you to add more to your wealth. This will give you the choice of taking on less risk to achieve your financial plan and the cash flow you need to achieve financial independence, or, if independent, to grow new wealth and increase your cash flow.

The CakeClub Way Of Thinking

Our philosophy, approach, and methodology are aimed at ensuring that you are going to have the highest probability of achieving the short- and long-term investment return objectives or percent return you require for your financial plan, at the lowest possible risk. We believe in MPT and that a highly diversified portfolio is the least risky and best choice. You, along with your adviser, need to actively monitor the performance of your portfolio; your adviser is responsible for reporting clearly and accurately to you the gross and net investment performance of all management fees.

A sophisticated yet straightforward approach to investing is best. Saving and wealth building is a journey that goes smoothest when you know both your destination and when you'd like to arrive there—the amount that you're building toward and the number of years you have to get there.

Once a clear destination and desired time frame are established, you can effectively develop and manage an investment portfolio that is focused on achieving your specific goals.

Sophisticated institutional investors understand this; that's why their approach to investing is to include portfolio holdings designed to generate, over the long term, the average annual return required to reach their goal within the planned time frame. Most individual investors err by not taking these steps first. As a result, many of them become overly preoccupied with building a portfolio that they feel will generate a return exceeding that of the S&P 500 index.

How We Measure Success

We believe that the correct way to measure success in wealth building is to gauge whether you remain on track to reaching your desired wealth goal in the planned time period, not the actual average annual rate of return you achieve.

Sophisticated investors recognize that anything else is just a distraction. Perhaps you have a goal of earning 6 percent a year; there will be years you're going to be above that and years you'll be below it. What matters is that you are achieving your financial plan at the least possible risk.

When you're looking for an investment adviser, we suggest an independent, registered investment adviser (RIA). That means that you want a professional who is only going to make decisions in your best interests. If you are not using an RIA, you are most likely using a broker. Brokers aren't held to as high a fiduciary standard. If you want to get unbiased advice based on what is in your best interests, always choose an independent RIA, especially one who finds money managers or funds for you and does not offer proprietary funds (ones they own) or receive any compensation from a money manager. The only fee your adviser should be receiving is from you.

Passive Versus Active Management

While this is not a book on investing, we should talk a little about another aspect of investment approach: passive versus active investment management.

Passive management is usually investing in index funds. An index fund follows the market of that fund. It is normally low-cost and relatively easy to invest in but doing so can result in higher taxes, and risk can also be higher. Due to just achieving the index return, when fees are deducted, it can result in you always underperforming the index. Also, you still have to decide on asset classes, allocation, and rebalancing the allocation to manage risk.

An active management approach means that your adviser selects managers who buy and sell securities based on their analyses and do not just follow an index. An adviser may also select individual securities. While their performance may be compared to an index, they will perform differently from the index. They may perform higher or lower, but you do have the chance to outperform the index. Fees are normally higher. It can be more complicated, but tax efficiency is normally better, and risk can be managed more effectively.

The ongoing debate is which management style performs better over time. Passive tends to be a better performer in rapidly rising markets, while active tends to perform better in a more volatile market. Over the long term, they tend to perform the same. We at CakeClub believe that there are good points in both ways of investing, and we advocate having a blend.

There are certain parts of the market where it's better to use a passive investment or index approach because of the costs, or because there's not much opportunity there. This is normally in large company stocks or international markets. We think that when it comes to smaller companies, it is much better to have individual securities because there are more and greater opportunities for active managers.

We've seen investment advisers who are proponents of passive investing, but they don't really talk about risk. To us, risk management is a necessary component of portfolio management and possibly could be better managed in an actively managed portfolio. We also find that there are more opportunities to save tax dollars with an actively managed portfolio, since you can sell individual securities and not just a portion of a fund. In our portfolio approach, we use technology to watch how active managers buy and sell. By watching and employing software, we think you might be able to add between a fraction of a percent up to 2 percent or more annually on the return of a portfolio.

There are other advantages for active management: Executives who work for large companies may have a concentrated holding in the securities of their own company and don't want any more in that particular company or industry. Active management can avoid adding those securities, whereas you would have to accept them as part of the holdings in an index fund.

We've had clients who, for either religious reasons or on principle, don't want to invest in what we call the "sin stocks": tobacco, gambling, or alcohol. We can remove those from a portfolio, which is normally impossible when buying into nonspecific index funds. Other clients have environmental, social, or political concerns and don't want to invest in companies they feel violate their principles.

Ask About The Reporting Process

When interviewing your potential investment adviser or talking with the one you already have, make sure that you clearly understand the reports on performance you receive. As the saying goes, "Trust, but verify." Verification ensures that you are on track with your Wealth Building Formula and your financial plan and that your investments are earning the percent return you need.

You should receive, at the very least, a quarterly report on your portfolio that allows you to track what your rate of return has been for that particular quarter, year to date, and since inception in absolute dollars, gross and net of management fees. Performance should also be reported as a percentage, both before and after management fees. That allows you to see what you have actually earned and what you are paying.

Too many brokerage houses and managers issue reports that are confusing or do not provide that amount of detail. That makes it tough to know if you're on track with your Wealth Building Formula or are on the right path to achieving your goals. By the way, it's not because they can't do this; the technology is there. These companies simply don't want to have to disclose all their fees and fee arrangements to you. You should demand this; it's what a well-run company would do, and your aim should be to run your personal finances in the same fashion. Demand accountability and clear documentation.

Your actual percent return, in part, is going to determine if you reach your short-term goals, how long you have to work, how much wealth you have, and the cash flow that can be produced from that wealth. It will determine what level of risk you might have to take. As we laid out in the ground rules, it's up to you to decide how involved in the process you wish to be. But if you're not paying attention, be prepared to make do with whatever the market produces for you—not what you could have produced.

So far, we've talked chiefly about building wealth. Now we're going to switch gears and discuss how to protect it for your loved ones or future generations, if that is important for you.

CakeClub Slices

- Know the long-term investment return objective (*%Return*) of your Wealth Building Formula.
- If using an investment adviser, make sure they have a philosophy, approach, and methodology that is aligned with your risk profile.
- Ensure you can read the investment reports sent to you. If not, demand that your adviser explain until you know how.
- Your adviser, fund, or brokerage company should be providing monthly, if not quarterly, portfolio reports. Review them.
- Know what your investment return is before and after management fees.
- Ensure you meet with your adviser at least once per year to review your risk preferences.

11

Estate Planning
Protecting What You Have Built

Only put off until tomorrow what you
are willing to die having left undone.
—Pablo Picasso, painter

Estate planning is one of the clearest expressions of responsibility. It is how you protect the people you love, reduce confusion, and make sure your wishes are carried out when you are no longer able to explain them yourself. It is not only for the wealthy. It is for anyone whose absence would leave decisions, burdens, or uncertainty behind.

Whether through your own diligent saving efforts, inheritance, or the lottery, you have or will have wealth—and hopefully more wealth than you'll need or want to spend in your life. What do you want to accomplish with your wealth, now or beyond your lifetime, for the people and causes you love?

Not everyone communicates love in the same way, and likewise, people have different ways they prefer to receive love. The concept of love languages was developed by Gary Chapman, PhD, in his book *The 5 Love Languages: The Secret to Love That Lasts*, in which he describes five unique styles of communicating love, categories he distilled from his experience in marriage counseling and linguistics.[50]

The five love languages are five different ways of expressing and receiving love: words of affirmation, quality time, acts of service, physical touch, and giving of gifts.

You don't do estate planning for you; you do it for your loved ones. Love is ensuring that those family members and causes you leave behind are looked after.

What Kind Of Legacy Do You Wish To Leave?

Perhaps you want to be sure that in the event of your passing, your spouse is secure in the same lifestyle you're enjoying together now or that your other loved ones—children and grandchildren—will have the opportunities in life that money can provide. You may wish to accomplish something else with your money, such as giving it to charity or a school.

However, if you don't put together a will or the other estate-planning documents that establish your wishes legally, the people who will likely determine what happens to your money will be your state government or the courts. Estate planning is also a way to preserve wealth and cash flow from avoidable taxation.

There are some real horror stories out there about people who should have been savvy enough to have planned adequately for their estates but failed to do so. When the heir to the Wrigley chewing gum fortune died, his estate planning was so deficient that his estate paid tens of millions of dollars to the government. The family had owned the Chicago Cubs for generations, but because of this planning failure, they had to sell the team to pay their tax bills. Experts who reviewed their estate documents subsequently said that this catastrophe was completely avoidable.

Keep in mind that we're not talking about adding wealth at this point; we're looking at strategies to preserve your wealth for your loved ones and for generations beyond that. If you don't have any family or any desire to contribute to society beyond your lifetime, and you do have a strong desire to hand your estate over to Uncle Sam, you can skip this chapter—but most of us do care about what we leave behind.

The Documents You Must Have And Should Have

The first document you want in an adequate estate plan is a will.

A properly written will can accomplish a few basic wishes for you. First, you will determine who will be in charge of seeing that your wishes, as expressed in your will, are carried out. That's your executor.

Second, you're going to determine how you wish your estate to be distributed. If you have minor children, you're going to determine whom you would like to act as guardians if you pass away before they've reached majority age.

A will is the primary estate instrument, but there are other documents you should have in order as well, depending on your circumstances. You might create what is called an irrevocable life insurance trust (ILIT). Placing life insurance into a trust will save estate taxes.

In any case, you should have a medical care directive or a living will. This will direct your medical care when you are unable to make those decisions. You might also consider other documents, like a limited power of attorney or a durable power of attorney. These documents allow trusted people you select to make decisions for you if you are unable to do so for yourself.

Various types of trusts can also be established during your lifetime or upon your passing that can fulfill your intentions and ensure that the government receives the least amount of taxes possible. Without these crucial documents in place, the government could step in and decide what is best for you or your loved ones and who gets your hard-earned money.

A limited power of attorney or a durable power of attorney comes into play in a situation in which you are temporarily incapacitated but are expected to recover. We had a client, an attorney, who resisted doing this; within weeks after he finally got this document done, he was in a car accident with his wife that left them both hospitalized, and they could not manage their financial affairs. They could not sign checks. They could not conduct certain business transactions. A limited power of attorney will give the people whom you designate the power to write checks or do limited transactions for you as you recover.

A durable power of attorney is broader, granting the person named the rights to do more extensive financial chores for you. Most people want a limited power of attorney because they want the designee to be able to handle their affairs, but they don't want them to be empowered to sell their home or make similar major decisions for which they'd want to give consent.

Estate planning is eventually an important part of your comprehensive personal financial plan. As part of our work with people, we urge a review of every aspect of estate planning and advise where action should be taken to make sure your estate is in good order, down to what kinds of insurance you have. We do this either to make sure your loved ones are taken care of and other legacy wishes are accomplished or, once you have exhausted every possible means of sheltering your estate, to pay whatever kind of estate taxes that you might owe.

Nobody Wants To Think About It

We find that for most people, estate planning is the last on the list of things to do. Maybe they don't want to admit to themselves that they're going to die or want to make decisions about who gets what or who's going to be in charge.

But honestly, that's a little selfish when you stop to consider the burden this places on your spouse, siblings, parents, or friends. Will they step in to help? Will anyone know what to do?

Yet most people spend more time selecting the toppings to order on a pizza than thinking about planning for their estate. Many who have spent the time to create a simple will may find that eventually it's not adequate to preserve the wealth they have built during their lives or to protect their loved ones in the event of sudden death. You may assume that your spouse can handle it all, but what if you're in an accident and your spouse is with you? It may not be enough just to rely on a will.

Taxes And Trusts

When people think about what they want to have happen to their wealth when they pass, they nearly always want to avoid taxes. They also wish to have some control.

In order to accomplish those aims, you might consider establishing trusts. This may allow you to take advantage of the exemptions the government gives you and allow that wealth to continue to grow outside of your estate, avoiding estate taxes. As mentioned earlier, placing your life insurance into an ILIT allows you to determine where you want the funds to go and also removes it from your estate and taxation.

You may explore other types of trusts to set up; one type to consider is called a spousal lifetime access trust (SLAT). This allows you to put the federal exemption amount for you and your spouse into a trust. As of this writing, this is $15 million per spouse. This allows that money to grow free of estate tax, out of your estate, and to future generations. A great feature of these particular trusts is that both spouses can have access to the funds during their lifetimes, if needed.

Another instrument is a grantor retained annuity trust (GRAT). This trust allows you to put assets in now and to receive income from these assets for a certain period as an annual payment from the trust. When you pass, any assets remaining will be turned over to your beneficiary—usually a close family member—as a gift.

Another strategy is called a qualified terminable interest property (QTIP). It's meant to take advantage of a marital deduction to control the ultimate distribution of assets after the death of both spouses. Simply put, for estate purposes, any property that passes to a current spouse is not subject to gift or estate tax. However, the whole property must pass to the current spouse. The transfer through a QTIP is an exception, as long as the current spouse has lifetime interest in the property.

QTIPs are commonly used when a spouse has children from another marriage. The spouse bringing the property into the marriage may wish to provide for this new spouse for their lifetime and take advantage of their unified tax credit, but nonetheless designate where the money goes after the new spouse is deceased. A QTIP allows this to be accomplished.

All of these are complex instruments that change all of the time. Depending on your specific situation, there could be many options to explore. Knowing which best serves your needs is most soundly decided by working with a very knowledgeable wealth adviser or estate-planning attorney. We would strongly advise against just using websites like LegalZoom.com for your estate planning, other than for simple wills.

Lastly, some words of advice: Don't be in a hurry to give away your estate. Make sure you have assets that generate the cash flow you need for your lifetime. This may not apply to you for many years, but we knew of a situation in which a very wealthy couple transferred assets to trusts for their children. Due to unforeseen circumstances, the children wound up with great wealth, while the parents' wealth decreased drastically and left them dependent on the children.

It's important to make sure that you have experts working with you to help you sort through the ramifications of your choices and to tell you what you need to prepare. As in all cases when using an expert, make sure they are of "championship" caliber.

CakeClub Slices

- Estate planning is one of the clearest expressions of responsibility.
- You don't do estate planning for you; you do it for your loved ones. If you don't have much to leave, and don't have a spouse or significant other, don't waste time and money on this right now, or make up a simple will.
- Even if you don't have much to leave, consider a medical directive or living will, and a durable or limited power of attorney, in the event of a medical emergency.
- Simple estate documents can be created using a low-cost online legal documents service but for more complex estates use a competent estate attorney.

12

Creating A Championship Team

Achieving the lifestyle you want now and in the future
is a lot easier when you surround yourself with
a championship-caliber team of experts.
—Albert J. Zdenek, Jr., CPA/PFS,
and Amin Boroomand, PhD

No one makes every major financial decision alone. At different moments in life, you may rely on an accountant, attorney, banker, insurance professional, investment adviser, or other specialist. The quality of those relationships matters. Good advisers do more than answer isolated questions. They understand your larger plan, communicate clearly, and help your decisions work together rather than compete with one another.

You make financial choices each day, and there are experts that you depend on for prudent advice and guidance. It's critical that these experts know what the plan is: What lifestyle do you wish to lead, now and in the future? What are your values? What is important to you?

If your advisers do not know these answers, they will not be able to steer you in the right direction, no matter their level of expertise. Your current accountant, attorney, banker, insurance agent, pension expert, and others may not know you or may not be working together as they should be to obtain the best results for you. They could be individual players, playing their own games, making decisions based on what they do for everyone else, rather than on the game plan for you or what you need.

You Don't Need To Be An Expert

You do not need to become a CPA, attorney, or any sort of expert yourself. However, the better you select the "players" on your team—a team that knows the overall game plan and has been tailored to your needs—the better financial choices you'll be able to make and the better chance you'll have to achieve the wealth and cash flow you need to live the life you want, now and forever.

How should your team of experts work? We use the Yankees as an example, even though Al is a Phillies fan. While the Steinbrenner family still owns the Yankees today, when George Steinbrenner was the owner of the Yankees (1973 to 2010), they were in the playoffs or in contention almost every year. Many times, they were world champions. Steinbrenner was aggressive in making sure that the very best players were on that team in their proper positions. Having the best players always guaranteed that the team was going to be competitive. Look to building your expert team with the same idea.

Most of us are far less intentional when we build our teams; they just seem to happen. We get a car, so we obtain car insurance. We probably use the agent our parents used or a college friend who's selling insurance. As needs arise, we add other players, but we don't always look at changing the ones we have, even as our needs become more complicated or demand more sophistication.

If you build yourself a championship team of experts, you have the best chance of achieving what you want. Anything less lessens that likelihood. Anything less could mean that you work longer and harder in life, that you make poor financial choices, and that you and your loved ones may not live the way you wish.

How Do You Know You Have Championship Team Players?

You may never know how much knowledge an expert has, but you can see the way the experts and their staff treat you. Do they return your phone calls in a timely fashion? When they promise to complete work in a certain time frame, do they do so? Or are they always late, requiring you to call them? When you're dealing with their staff, whether it's their receptionist or the people who assist them, are you being treated with friendly, high-touch service? Do they care about important events in your life? Do they know the names of your children? Is your expert proactive? Do they call you once in a while, not because you called them but because they thought of an idea for you?

The main way you can judge your experts is by how you are treated by them and their staff. If you are not getting proactive service, promptly returned calls, or work completed properly and on time, maybe you're not getting the best services.

You have a choice. You can change players, or instead of having an A team, you can keep your B or C team players. If you have B team players, you'll have a B team financial plan, you'll have B team financial help or guidance, and there's a greater chance that you're going to work longer in life, you're not going to have as much as you should have, and you're not going to live the life you wish. If you have an A team, it's more likely that you're going to build what you want in life, you're going to live life the way you want, and you're going to be able to accomplish what you want.

The Role Of The Wealth Adviser

You are the team owner. You pay them, and they do what you want. You create the plan to "win the championship" (your financial plan) with the "coach" you hire (your wealth adviser). We urge you to rate the experts that work with you. If we ever see a B or C player, we let our clients know. If we get any comment from a client other than, "They're terrific," we tell them that it may be time to look around for someone else.

It's a big red flag when a person says, "Well, Joshua's been my insurance agent since I got out of college twenty-five years ago, and he's a good old boy," or anything like that. Our question is, "OK, what has Joshua done for you recently?" We find out that the only time the client is in contact with Joshua, besides going golfing or fishing, is when he thinks of a need, and he calls Joshua.

Reality check: If you're coming up with or are reading about better ideas than the people on your expert list have, you'd better start to replace them. If you have your own business, you know that you have some A, B, and C players as employees. The surest road to ruin for a business is to have C players on the payroll. B employees may not be that much better. When it comes to your team of experts, if you don't have all A players, you're not going to be able to accomplish what you could have, and it's going to be a longer struggle for you.

Having a championship team in place helps our clients make the best financial decisions for themselves, build and preserve the wealth they need, and manage it more effectively. As a result, they sleep better at night than those people who have a subpar team.

During times of emergency or uncertainty, this is even more important. When the market's not doing well or things are going wrong in your life—if there's an unexpected death or an illness, you lose your job, or your business is going through terrible times—a championship team is an invaluable asset.

Don't let sentiment, habit, or being busy keep you from assembling the best team you possibly can. Your financial life and those of your loved ones literally depend on it.

CakeClub Slices

- Create your own championship team of advisers.
- If you have some advisers who are not championship-level, replace them with better ones.
- Meet with your advisers at least once per year and review how they helped you (or not) the past year.
- Track how much they save or cost you with their advice.

In Closing . . .

I feel that luck is preparation meeting opportunity.
—Seneca the Younger, philosopher

Changing your financial life does not happen all at once. It happens one decision at a time. One clearer number. One better question. One avoided mistake. One repeated habit.

If this book has done its job, you should now feel less intimidated by money and more capable of directing it. You do not need to know everything today. You do need to begin.

Start where you are. Look honestly at what is true. Decide what kind of life you want. Then make your next financial choice in a way that supports that life. Do that often enough, and your future will begin to change.

Sometimes, the first steps to transform your life are the most difficult. Just take the first step.

Resources For Your Next Step

www.CakeClubapp.com

The CakeClub app
CakeClub's AI Assistant in the CakeClub app

Contact Information

Amin Boroomand, PhD
CEO
CakeClub Inc.
510-813-8790
Amin@cakeclubapp.com

Albert J. Zdenek, Jr., CPA/PFS
Executive Chairman
CakeClub Inc.
908-797-4601
Al@cakeclubapp.com

Acknowledgments

A book is part of a journey in life. Like the log of a ship, it records only part of the journey. As such, there are many people who help make this trip a success and certainly a lot smoother than if we had planned it totally by ourselves.

Journeys take financial backing. Thank you to those who had faith in CakeClub Inc. and this publication. As of this writing, these include Dr. Hershey and Marianne Bell, Dr. Charles A. and Monica Accurso, Frank and Shirley Bonner, Nancy Smalley-Sullivan, Kenneth A. McCord, Jr., and The Pont des Arts Trust, who wished to be part of a legacy of people being educated to make the best financial decisions, live the life they want along the way, and achieve financial freedom in the time frame they want.

Many contributed their talents in other ways. We thank Rich Cancro, Dr. David Zelman, Mohsen Sharifani, Ashley Montazer, Amir Arsalan Khalilian, Al Sterling, Andrew Gray, Louis Tzamalas, and Sejdo Radoncic for generously sharing their time and knowledge.

A great amount of appreciation goes to Henry DeVries and Jazmin Barnes of Wealth Authority Books. Their expert guidance and caring advice in the writing and editing added a tremendous amount of value to this book.

Albert J. Zdenek Sr. and Rose Marie Prince Zdenek were unconditional, loving, and inspirational parents to Al. There is not a day that goes by that some memory or lesson of theirs does not give Al wise guidance and happiness.

Amin lovingly acknowledges his parents, Karim and Mina, whose love, sacrifice, and constant presence became the quiet foundation beneath so much of his journey.

We acknowledge Alain Briscadieu-Farjas and Dr. Hannah Hickman, who supported us with love, patience, and remarkable tolerance for distracted partners, stolen hours, and endless "just one more thing" moments. Without them, this book may have been finished earlier, but it would have contained fewer hard-earned financial lessons, less depth, and far less heart.

About The Authors

Albert J. Zdenek, Jr., CPA/PFS

Al Zdenek is a financial strategist, entrepreneur, and longtime adviser with more than four decades of experience helping individuals and families make better financial decisions. His work has focused on wealth building, cash flow management, and helping people align financial choices with the lives they want to live.

He is the executive chairman of CakeClub Inc. and the former president, chief executive officer, and founder of Traust Sollus Wealth Management LLC, in New York City.

Al is the author of Amazon best-selling books *Master Your Cash Flow: The Key to Grow And Retain Wealth* (ForbesBooks, 2017) and *Master Your Business Cash Flow: Grow the Company You Love, Live the Life You Want Now* (ForbesBooks, 2018).

He holds a BA from Rutgers College and an MBA from Rutgers Graduate School of Business. His hobbies include traveling, wine, cooking, and reading. He spends time teaching and mentoring.

Al is an aspiring pianist and enjoys living in Miami and Paris.

Amin Boroomand, PhD

Amin Boroomand, PhD, is a serial entrepreneur, and as CEO, is the visionary force behind the founding of CakeClub Inc., a personal finance company and creator of the CakeClub app. "Financial Freedom for Everyone" is the mission of CakeClub.

Amin's path has taken him across disciplines, industries, and continents, from agricultural engineering to bioinformatics to computational social science, always driven by one core question: Where can knowledge create the greatest real-world impact? He found his answer in personal finance.

Despite years of advanced education and analytical training, he experienced firsthand the challenge of navigating finances without guidance. Amin realized how little financial education most people actually receive, how poorly they make financial decisions, that they were not living the life they wanted, and how deeply money-related stress harmed everyday life. He had a vision to change the world.

Amin joined forces with wealth management pioneer Al Zdenek. Together, they set out to combine Al's decades of proprietary and successful financial processes with Amin's cutting-edge perspective on technology, product development, and behavioral science to build an app that was both practical and transformative: a smarter, more human approach to financial freedom.

Previously, Amin advised CEOs in biotech and other high-tech sectors and helped shape successful ventures through market research, customer discovery, business model design, and innovation strategy.

His doctoral research at the University of California, Merced, explored how risk-taking, team diversity, and clarity of communication shape performance in complex problem-solving, themes that continue to shape his approach to leadership, product design, and decision-making.

He has also served as an adviser and board member to many emerging technology companies. An Iranian American, Amin was educated across Iran, Italy, and the United States. He brings a global perspective to leadership, innovation, and resilience. He was recognized by MIT Technology Review as one of its "Innovators Under 35" (TR35) in Italy, and his entrepreneurial work has been recognized in international competitions, including Berlin Startup Ideas and Expo Milan.

What defines Amin's work is not just technical depth or entrepreneurial range, but a strong belief that meaningful innovation begins with understanding people. He is especially interested in decision-making, human behavior, storytelling, and building products that genuinely improve lives.

He also has a long-standing love of stand-up comedy.

Author's Notes And Works Cited

1 Joint Center for Housing Studies of Harvard University, "The State of the Nation's Housing 2025," (Harvard University, 2025), https://www.jchs.harvard.edu/sites/default/files/reports/files/Harvard_JCHS_The_State_of_the_Nations_Housing_2025.pdf.

2 U.S. Bureau of Labor Statistics. Consumer Price Index for All Urban Consumers: Rent of Primary Residence in U.S. City Average [CUUR0000SEHA], retrieved from Federal Reserve Bank of St. Louis, accessed March 31, 2026, https://fred.stlouisfed.org/data/CUUR0000SEHA. U.S. Census Bureau. Real Median Household Income in the United States [MEHOINUSA672N], retrieved from Federal Reserve Bank of St. Louis, accessed March 31, 2026, https://fred.stlouisfed.org/data/MEHOINUSA672N.

3 Federal Student Aid, "Federal Student Aid Posts Updated Reports to FSA Data Center (GENERAL-26-15)," U.S. Department of Education, March 13, 2026, https://fsapartners.ed.gov/knowledge-center/library/electronic-announcements/2026-03-13/federal-student-aid-posts-updated-reports-fsa-data-center.

4 Jennifer Ma et al., "Trends in College Pricing and Student Aid 2025," (College Board, 2025), accessed March 31, 2026, https://research.collegeboard.org/media/pdf/Trends-in-College-Pricing-and-Student-Aid-2025-final_1.pdf.

5 "Federal Reserve Board - Consumer Credit - G.19," accessed April 2, 2026, https://www.federalreserve.gov/releases/g19/hist/cc_hist_tc_levels.html.

6 Benjamin Graham, *The Intelligent Investor* (Harper, 1949).

7 Paul Sullivan, "The Bad Fortune of Some Ultrawealthy People," NYT, December 12, 2015, p. B4, https://www.nytimes.com/2015/12/12/your-money/the-bad-fortune-of-some-ultrawealthy-people.html.

8 "Report on the Economic Well-Being of U.S. Households in 2024 - May 2025," Board of Governors of the Federal Reserve System, accessed March 31, 2026, https://www.federalreserve.gov/publications/2025-economic-well-being-of-us-households-in-2024-savings-and-investments.htm.

9 Gallup, Inc., "State of the Global Workplace: 2022 Report," 2022, https://web.millennium-challenge.com/wp-content/uploads/2023/01/state-of-the-global-workplace-2022-download-1.pdf.

10 "Consumer Insights on Managing Spending," Consumer Financial Protection Bureau, February 28, 2017, https://www.consumerfinance.gov/data-research/research-reports/consumer-insights-managing-spending/.

11 Talker Research newsroom, "Multiple Jobs to Cold Showers: How Gen Z Tries to Survive the Economy," Talker Research, January 7, 2026, https://talkerresearch.com/multiple-jobs-to-cold-showers-how-gen-z-tries-to-survive-the-economy/.

12 OverDrive, "Libraries Break Digital Lending Records in 2025 With Over 820 Million Checkouts and Over 1 Billion Minutes Streamed," press release, January 22, 2026, https://company.overdrive.com/2026/01/21/libraries-break-digital-lending-records-in-2025-with-over-820-million-checkouts-and-over-1-billion-minutes-streamed/.

13 P. M. Gollwitzer and P. Sheeran, "Implementation Intentions and Goal Achievement: A Meta-Analysis of Effects and Processes," *Advances in Experimental Social Psychology* 38, (2006), 69–119.

14 K. L. Milkman et al., "Holding the Hunger Games Hostage at the Gym: An Evaluation of Temptation Bundling," *Management Science* 60, no. 2 (2014), 283–99.

15 *Downton Abbey*, season 1, episode 2, "Episode Two," written by Julian Fellowes, directed by Ben Bolt, aired October 3, 2010, on ITV.

16 J. Ameriks et al., "Wealth Accumulation and the Propensity to Plan," *The Quarterly Journal of Economics* 118, no. 3 (August 1, 2003): 1007–47, https://doi.org/10.1162/00335530360698487.

17 Heart Mind Strategies, "Consumer Views on Personal Cash Flow Planning," CFP Board, January 2019, https://www.cfp.net/-/media/files/cfp-board/knowledge/reports-and-research/consumer-surveys/consumer-views-on-cash-flow-planning-january-2019.pdf.

18 R. H. Thaler and S. Benartzi, "Save More Tomorrow™: Using Behavioral Economics to Increase Employee Saving," *Journal of Political Economy* 112, no. S1 (2004), S164–S187.

19 Thaler and Benartzi, "Save More Tomorrow™."

20 B. C. Madrian and D. F. Shea, "The Power of Suggestion: Inertia in 401(k) Participation and Savings Behavior," *Quarterly Journal of Economics* 116, no. 4 (2001), 1149–87.

21 "Financial Well-Being: The Goal of Financial Education," Consumer Financial Protection Bureau, August 8, 2023, https://www.consumerfinance.gov/data-research/research-reports/financial-well-being/.

22 Anandi Mani et al., "Poverty Impedes Cognitive Function," *Science* 341, no. 6149 (August 29, 2013): 976–80, https://doi.org/10.1126/science.1238041.

23 American Psychological Association, "APA Survey Shows Money Stress Weighing on Americans' Health Nationwide," press release, February 4, 2015, https://www.apa.org/news/press/releases/2015/02/money-stress.

24 Rand D. Conger, Katherine J. Conger, and Monica J. Martin, "Socioeconomic Status, Family Processes, and Individual Development," *Journal of Marriage and Family* 72, no. 3 (June 2010): 685–704, https://doi.org/10.1111/j.1741-3737.2010.00725.x.

25 Better Money Habits, "Personal Finance Education & Tips from Better Money Habits," Better Money Habits, December 17, 2025, https://bettermoneyhabits.bankofamerica.com/en.

26 "Confronted With Higher Living Costs, 72% of Young Adults Take Action to Improve Their Financial Health, Finds BofA Better Money Habits Study," Bank of America, July 30, 2025, https://newsroom.bankofamerica.com/content/newsroom/press-releases/2025/07/confronted-with-higher-living-costs--72--of-young-adults-take-ac.html.

27 Better Money Habits, "Personal Finance Education."

28 R. H. Thaler, "Mental Accounting Matters," *Journal of Behavioral Decision Making* 12, no. 3 (1999), 183–206.

29 Nathan Boole, "Subscription Service Statistics and Costs," C+R Research, last updated July 26, 2024, https://www.crresearch.com/blog/subscription-service-statistics-and-costs/.

30 Boole, "Subscription Service Statistics."

31 Suzanne Blake, "Gen Z Has a Serious Debt Problem," *Newsweek*, February 9, 2024, https://www.newsweek.com/gen-z-struggling-pay-debt-student-loans-1868611.

32 "Credit Union and Bank Rates 2025 Q3," NCUA, September 26, 2025, https://ncua.gov/analysis/cuso-economic-data/credit-union-bank-rates/credit-union-and-bank-rates-2025-q3.

33 National Credit Union Administration, "NCUA Board Extends Loan Interest Rate Ceiling," press release, NCUA, February 6, 2026, https://ncua.gov/newsroom/press-release/2026/ncua-board-extends-loan-interest-rate-ceiling.

34 "Consumer Credit - G.19," Board of Governors of the Federal Reserve System, accessed March 31, 2026, https://www.federalreserve.gov/releases/g19/hist/cc_hist_tc_levels.html.

35 Rachel Hale, "Gen Z Is 'Financial Flexing.' Why They're Going Broke to Look Successful," *USA TODAY*, updated December 4, 2025, https://www.usatoday.com/story/life/health-wellness/2025/12/03/gen-z-is-going-broke-to-look-rich-on-tiktok-and-instagram/87372477007/.

36 A.N. Thorndike et al., "Traffic-Light Labels and Choice Architecture: Promoting Healthy Food Choices," *American Journal of Preventive Medicine* 46, no. 2 (2014), 143–49.

37 L. Schomburgk et al., "Less Cash, More Splash? A Meta-Analysis on the Cashless Effect," *Journal of Retailing* 100, no. 3 (2024), 382–403.

38 "Subscription Spending Statistics (2026): What the Data Shows," ReSubs, March 16, 2026, https://resubs.app/resources/subscription-spending-statistics.

39 "Cost of Unused Subscriptions 2025," Self, November 21, 2025, https://www.self.inc/info/cost-of-unused-paid-subscriptions/.

40 Stephanie Prange, "Home Entertainment Forecast 2026: Streaming Flexes Its Muscle, Transactional a Critical Revenue Bridge," Media Play News, January 19, 2026, https://www.mediaplaynews.com/home-entertainment-forecast-2026-streaming-flexes-its-muscle-transactional-a-critical-revenue-bridge/.

41 Giles Tongue, "One in Three Americans Are Cutting Household Costs to Hang on to Their Streaming Subscriptions," Bango, November 5, 2025, https://bango.com/one-in-three-americans-are-cutting-household-costs-to-hang-on-to-their-streaming-subscriptions/.

42 "2025 Digital Media Trends: Social Platforms Are Becoming a Dominant Force in Media and Entertainment," Deloitte Insights, December 24, 2025, https://www.deloitte.com/us/en/insights/industry/technology/digital-media-trends-consumption-habits-survey/2025.html.

43 Please take a look at the following links for more supporting statistics: https://brokerlistings.com/research-hub/subscription-economy and https://www.self.inc/info/cost-of-unused-paid-subscriptions/.

44 Boole, "Subscription Service Statistics."

45 Gollwitzer, "Implementation Intentions and Goal Achievement."

46 Dilip Soman and Amar Cheema, "Earmarking and Partitioning: Increasing Saving by Low-Income Households," *Journal of Marketing Research* 48, no. SPL (February 1, 2011): S14–22, https://doi.org/10.1509/jmkr.48.spl.s14.

47 "How Trust Drives Gen Z's Approach to Investing," World Economic Forum, January 16, 2026, https://www.weforum.org/stories/2026/01/gen-z-financial-investment-trust/.

48 Harry Markowitz, "Portfolio selection," The Journal of Finance, 7(1), 77–91, March 1952, https://doi.org/10.1111/j.1540-6261.1952.tb01525.x.

49 Nobel Prize Outreach, "The Prize in Economic Sciences 1990," NobelPrize.org, accessed March 31, 2026, https://www.nobelprize.org/prizes/economic-sciences/1990/press-release/.

50 Gary Chapman, T*he 5 Love Languages: The Secret to Love That Lasts* (Northfield Pub, 2015).

www.ingramcontent.com/pod-product-compliance
Lightning Source LLC
Chambersburg PA
CBHW031324230926
51848CB00001B/81